A GUIDE TO

SCIENCE AND BELIEF

M I C H A E L

P O O L E

A LION MANUAL
Oxford · Batavia · Sydney

Published by
Lion Publishing plc
Sandy Lane West, Oxford, England
ISBN 0 7459 1909 X
Lion Publishing Corporation
1705 Hubbard Avenue, Batavia, Illinois 60510, USA
ISBN 0 7459 1909 X
Albatross Books Pty Ltd
PO Box 320, Sutherland, NSW 2232, Australia
ISBN 0 7324 0243 3

First edition 1990

British Library Cataloguing in Publication Data
Poole, Michael
    A guide to science and belief.
    1. Religion related to science
    1. Title
    215

    ISBN 0–7459–1909–X

Library of Congress Cataloging-in-Publication Data
Poole, Michael (Michael W.)
    A guide to science and belief/Michael Poole.—1st ed.
    "A Lion manual."
    ISBN 0–7459–1909–X
    1. Religion and science—1946– 2. Faith. 1. Title
BL240.2.P62   1990   90–35853
261.5'5—dc20   CIP

Printed and bound in Yugoslavia

CONTENTS

FINDING ANSWERS

Do religion and science conflict? Is science the final test of what to believe?

How different are we from other animals? What are the six 'days' of creation?

Does science contradict the Bible? How do we understand the Bible?

Why did Galileo and the church collide? What did Galileo say about the Bible?

Do scientific explanations replace God? Isn't religious experience explained psychologically?

Is faith believing what you know isn't true? How do we know if God is real?

Does science rule out miracles? How does God work in the world?

Cosmic accident or God's design? Was the world created?

Is God really a 'father'? Is an atom really a 'solar system'?

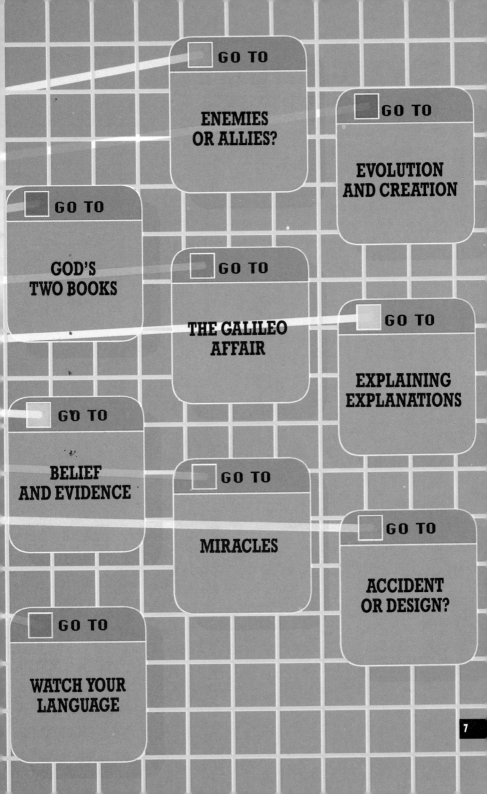

GO TO

ENEMIES OR ALLIES?

GO TO

EVOLUTION AND CREATION

GO TO

GOD'S TWO BOOKS

GO TO

THE GALILEO AFFAIR

GO TO

EXPLAINING EXPLANATIONS

GO TO

BELIEF AND EVIDENCE

GO TO

MIRACLES

GO TO

ACCIDENT OR DESIGN?

GO TO

WATCH YOUR LANGUAGE

SOME SCIENTISTS HAVE RELIGIOUS BELIEF

"There is but one God the father of whom are all things and we in him and one Lord Jesus Christ by whom are all things and we by him."

Sir Isaac Newton, who formulated the law of gravity

"Science is dealing with things that are given. Attitudes of awe, wonder, and humility before the facts are essential if man is to be in harmony with both his environment and his creator."

John Houghton, Director General of Britain's Meteorological Office

Professor Albert Einstein, who proposed the theories of relativity

"To the sphere of religion belongs the faith that the regulations valid for the world of existence are rational, that it is comprehensible to reason. I cannot conceive of a genuine scientist without that profound faith."

"Galileo, and the astronomers who came after him, dealt a blow to the Church from which it can never hope to recover."

Margaret Knight, who wrote *Morals without Religion*

"A miracle is a violation of the laws of nature . . . the proof against a miracle . . . is as entire as any argument from experience can possibly be imagined."

David Hume, philosopher

SOME PEOPLE THINK DIFFERENTLY

OF WHAT TO BELIEVE?

DO ITS LAWS MAKE BELIEF IN MIRACLES IMPOSSIBLE?

HAS THE WORK OF DARWIN RULED OUT THE IDEA OF A CREATING GOD?

"Darwin removed the idea of God as the Creator and gave a theory to enlightened and progressive thinkers."

Francis Hitching, presenter of television programmes for schools

THIS IS A RESOURCE BOOK OF IDEAS WHICH EXPLORES QUESTIONS LIKE THESE.

PART ONE: GOD'S 'TWO BOOKS'

How do we find out what the world is like? And how do we discover how it began?

Today, we turn immediately to science. Scientists can trace the origins of the earth, and the birth of the universe. They can unravel the mysteries of nature.

But for all the progress which science has made in the last two

centuries, there are questions scientists cannot answer—and never will be able to—questions like 'has the universe a purpose?' We need to find that out from somewhere else.

The development of modern science owes a great deal to Francis Bacon (1561–1626). He believed that God had 'spoken' in two great 'Books'. One was the 'Book of Nature'(the World) and the other was the 'Book of Scripture' (the Word). The first was about the Creation, the second was about the Creator. The first was seen as the 'Book of God's Works', the second as the 'Book of God's Words'.

So, if you wanted to find out what God had said, you 'read' the appropriate 'book'.

Looking at the world of nature only told you certain, scientific, things. You also needed the Bible for the complete picture.

"It being true that two truths cannot contradict one another, it is the function of wise expositors to seek out the true senses of scriptural texts. These will unquestionably accord with the physical conclusions which manifest sense and necessary demonstrations have previously made certain to us."
Galileo

The 'Book of Scripture' and the 'Book of Nature' were not expected to contradict each other.

The 'Book of Nature' and the 'Book of Scripture'—God's two ways of speaking to us. Understood like this, science and Christian belief are not expected to be in conflict, but to complement each other.

THE 'BOOK OF GOD'S WORDS'

There is more to understanding the Bible than simply reading off the face value of its words.

Galileo complained about people who tried to force astronomical theories out of the Bible. 'The intention of the Holy Ghost,' he quoted, 'is to teach us how one goes to heaven, not how heaven goes.'

To take a passage 'literally', if the passage was not intended that way, can lead to the kinds of wrangles Galileo became involved in. Psalm 93 compares the steadfastness of God to the world: 'The world is firmly established; it cannot be moved.' This

was taken by some of Galileo's opponents to mean the earth is stationary and theories of the earth orbiting the sun were wrong.

The Bible is full of passages which must not be read like a scientific journal. They use poetry or stories to make their point.

There is a big difference between 'literally' and 'literary'. Problems arise because it is not always easy to distinguish what is intended *literally* from what is a *literary* device.

Even those who say that they 'take the whole Bible literally', rarely do so. They recognize the poetry and imagery in expressions like, 'the morning stars sang together'.

"The material imagery has never been taken literally by anyone who had reached the stage when he could understand what 'taking it literally' meant."
Professor C.S.Lewis

"The world is firmly established; it cannot be moved."

The beauty and wonder of the earth and of space are conveyed in the Bible by striking poetic images.

1 WHAT'S IN THE BIBLE?

The Bible uses a wide range of ways to speak about God.

It includes poetry, proverbs, parables, epics, prophecy, history, prayers, songs, personal and circular letters, irony, paradoxes and jokes which play upon words. In short, the Bible is a collection of literary documents. To understand it, the *literary genre*—or style of writing—needs to be taken into account.

To say that parables, for example, are not historical does not downgrade them. It is no more sensible to look for historical or scientific statements in a text if the writers did not intend it, than it is to look *only* for spiritual meanings when the writers apparently intended to describe something historical as well. Some passages are historical, some are symbolic, and others are both.

ONE BOOK, MANY WRITINGS

Prophecy and revelation
After this I looked, and there before me was a door standing open in heaven. And the voice I had first heard speaking to me like a trumpet said, 'Come up here, and I will show you what must take place after this.'
Revelation 4:1

Laws and instructions
'When you reap the harvest of your land, do not reap to the very edges of your field or gather the gleanings of your harvest. Leave them for the poor and the alien.'
Leviticus 23:22

Parable
Jesus told them another parable:
The kingdom of heaven is like yeast that a woman took and mixed into a large amount of flour until it worked all through the dough.'
Matthew 13:33

Prayers
Our father in heaven, hallowed be your name, your kingdom come, your will be done on earth as it is in heaven.
Matthew 6:9–10

History
David son of Jesse was king over all Israel. He ruled Israel for forty years—seven in Hebron and thirty-three in Jerusalem.
1 Chronicles 29:26–27

Proverbs
He who guards his mouth and his tongue keeps himself from calamity.
Proverbs 21:23

Poetry and Songs
O Lord my God, you are very great; you are clothed with splendour and majesty.
He wraps himself in light as with a garment; he stretches out the heavens like a tent and lays the beams of his upper chambers on their waters.
Psalm 104:1–2

1 HOW DO WE UNDERSTAND THE BIBLE?

Careful study of the Bible involves trying to find out the original meaning of the text and determining its sense for modern readers. It takes into account:

■ **The cultural background of its readers.** What would *they* have understood by the passage?

■ **The attitudes, assumptions and intentions of the writers.** What were the writers trying to say, and what were their beliefs?

■ **The literary forms used.** Was the writer using poetry, or was he writing history? Is this a parable or a prayer?

It is misleading to think someone trying to understand a particular text comes with an entirely open mind, into which the text 'speaks'. A two-way process takes place. The questions which interpreters ask about the text are influenced by the assumptions they bring to their study. These 'presuppositions' are things taken for granted to be true, perhaps uncritically. They are affected by culture, what counts as 'common sense' and what is regarded as 'rational'.

Interpreters' presuppositions powerfully affect what they 'see' in the text and the answers they look for. These answers in turn affect their own views and hence shape subsequent questions. Sometimes the interpretations tell us more about the interpreter than the text.

"The interpreter's prior decision about the possibility or impossibility of miracle is bound to influence his conclusions about the historicity of the miracle stories even more than his literary analysis of the traditions."
Graham Stanton, Professor of New Testament Studies

According to the Bible's creation story, the animals were created 'after their kinds'. Does this necessarily mean that species were fixed for all time, and that no new species would develop?

THE 'KINDS' OF GENESIS

The effect of presuppositions is highlighted by a science-and-religion issue. In the Book of Genesis it says that God created everything 'after its own kind'. This can be read simply as saying that God acts in an orderly manner: dogs breed puppies, cats breed kittens and not snakes or bees.

But some people have read the text through the 'scientific spectacles' of our own culture. They have taken 'kinds' to mean the modern scientific term 'species', which is a reproductively isolated population, or group of populations. Those who do so feel obliged to try to defend the 'fixity of species' and oppose evolutionary theory. But it can be argued that this position arises from what they have *read into the text*—rather than read out of it.

"The Biblical creation narratives must not be used as a *scientific* account. They are concerned with theological truths. This is not to impute inaccuracy, but to insist upon the purpose of the passages."
Sam Berry, Professor of Genetics

"Twentieth-century Western culture seems to me particularly inept at understanding and using figurative or symbolic literature. We are so accustomed to straightforward, matter-of-fact descriptive prose that we expect nearly all writing to be of that form . . . Scientific writing has made an illegitimate claim of superiority over artistic literature."
Howard Van Till, Professor of Physics and Astronomy

Reading into the text can create imaginary enemies. It is rather like the shadow-boxer who creates imaginary opponents and then feels obliged to attack them.

In the arguments between science and religion the real focus is often on how the Bible is to be understood. Many of the apparent conflicts disappear when the Bible is understood on its own terms rather than from a twentieth-century scientific outlook.

1 THE 'BOOK OF GOD'S WORKS'

It seems obvious to us today that if we want to discover something about our world we go out and do an experiment. Do bodies fall at speeds which depend on their masses? All we need to do is to time them falling from a high building.

This is not how it has always been. Before the coming of science as we know it, people would form an idea of how the world *should* be, and then work from the assumption that it was so. Since movement in a circle was thought to be 'the most perfect form of motion' then, it was assumed that all the planets and stars moved in circles around humanity on earth. It was obvious from the starting point of perfect motion. To find out something, all you needed to do was consult the ancient authorities, such as the Greek writer Aristotle.

Francis Bacon emphasized that, to understand the natural world, we must look at nature rather than the writings of Aristotle. After all, Aristotle said that life was impossible at the equator. But sailors disproved this by bringing back people from the tropics. Bacon's emphasis was a major shift in thinking. If it seems obvious today, that is only because the whole scientific tradition, within which we have grown up, is based upon it.

But Bacon's view of science first collecting facts and then making up theories to fit them is misleading. Usually the scientist already has some theory about what he or she is looking for—otherwise the data collecting would be endless! Scientists test their initial guesses against the natural world, and make generalizations in the form of scientific 'laws'.

So, understanding science, like understanding the Bible, involves much more than simply 'reading off' the 'Book of God's Works' at face value. We interpret in science, too, according to a complex web of existing ideas.

The heart of scientific work is experimentation.

1 THE BASIS OF SCIENCE

Science involves a number of basic beliefs about the world. These beliefs are not proved by science—they have to be accepted even to begin.

■ Rationality

Rationality implies that our thought processes make sense and are basically reliable. This presupposition is central to all branches of study. You cannot even discuss whether rationality is a valid assumption without committing yourself to the assumption that it is!

■ Intelligibility

Whereas rationality assumes we can make sense and understand, intelligibility assumes the world can be understood. If we did not believe that, there would be no point in trying to do science.

'What attracts young men and women to the study of the physical world, and holds them to it despite the weariness and frustration inherent in research, is the marvellous way in which that world is open to our understanding,' wrote Dr John Polkinghorne.

■ Orderliness

The belief that nature is orderly, that it is *cosmos*, not *chaos*, makes it worthwhile searching for patterns which can be summarized in scientific laws.

■ Uniformity

Belief in the uniformity of nature is the assumption that, even though the world changes, the underlying laws of nature remain the same in time and space. For example, although gravity has resulted in both the birth and the death of stars at different times, the law of gravity itself has remained the same.

■ Worthwhileness

Without the presupposition that science is a worthwhile and legitimate activity, people would not carry out experiments.

1 SELECTIVE SCIENCE

Many people believe science is the objective collecting of facts from which, by 'the Scientific Method', general laws are produced. But there is no one scientific method. There are many, and good fortune and lucky guesses play their part too.

Science is conducted by human beings. And all of us have our preferences, prejudices and politics. What we believe generally may affect the conclusions we come to about scientific experiments.

What happens is that something catches our interest, and we set out to make observations. But we already have some theory in mind about what data to collect. In experiments on falling objects, people do not bother to record the object's colours or ownership. Consciously or unconsciously, their theory has already made them reject such factors as irrelevant.

What we are looking for can powerfully affect what we 'see'. Someone looking for a book on a library shelf may bypass it many times if the cover happens to be blue when they were convinced it was red. Selective perception affects everybody. Unwelcome data, which do not fit in with a favourite theory, can easily be overlooked without intentional dishonesty.

We will return to this theme when we look at the debate over evolution and creation. Do our preferences make us pre-judge the scientific issues?

Scientists work within the framework of theories. This makes it hard to acknowledge results which challenge strongly-held ideas.

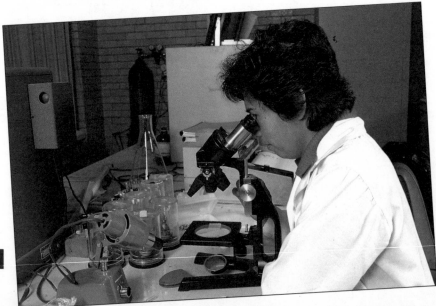

THE STORY OF HERTZ

In 1864 James Clerk Maxwell published his theory of how light travels. Nearly a quarter of a century later Hertz discovered radio waves, and wanted to know if radio waves behaved like Maxwell's light waves. For instance, did they both travel at the same speed?

In designing his experiment, Hertz believed that the size and colour of his laboratory did not matter. Radio waves would travel as fast on Monday as Sunday, in a blue room as well as a green one. Hertz already had a theory in mind, so he ignored what he thought of as irrelevant data. If he had brought no theory at all to his observations he would have needed to record a host of these obviously irrelevant facts like the colour of the apparatus and the size of the laboratory.

But convictions about what data are relevant can make scientists miss things which are significant.

Hertz obtained different values for the speeds of radio and light waves. This was opposite to what Maxwell's Electromagnetic Theory of Light predicted. After Hertz's death it was realized that radio waves reflected from the walls had interfered with his measurements. So the 'obviously irrelevant' size of the laboratory turned out to be very relevant.

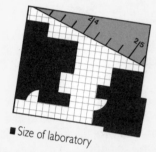
■ Size of laboratory

■ Speed of light

■ Colour of apparatus

■ Temperature and humidity

■ Day of the week

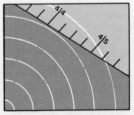
■ Distance travelled by radio waves

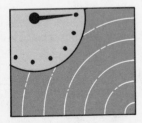
■ Times taken by radio waves

PART TWO: ENEMIES OR ALLIES?

For more than four centuries there has been a great deal of fruitful interaction between science and religious beliefs. But there have also been tensions, although these have often been exaggerated for the sake of controversy.

The impression frequently given by the mass media, for whom confrontation is news, is that science and religion are at loggerheads and scientists are automatically irreligious. But this is not the case:

"Sometimes people ask if religion and science are not opposed to one another. They are: in the sense that the thumb and fingers of my hand are opposed to one another. It is an opposition by means of which anything can be grasped."
Professor Sir William Bragg

"Science . . . religion . . . On the one hand there is the law of gravitation, and on the other the contemplation of the beauty of holiness. What one side sees, the other misses; and vice versa."
Professor A.N. Whitehead

"Science without religion is lame, religion without science is blind."
Professor Albert Einstein

Why can science without religion be said to be lame? One answer might be to point to the stimulus which the Christian faith provided for science to begin its meteoric rise. Far from being in opposition, religious belief encouraged science.

THE DEVELOPMENT OF SCIENCE

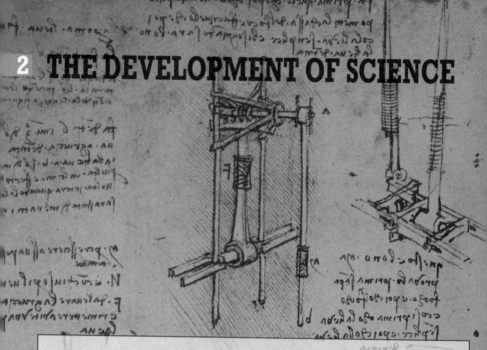

During the sixteenth and seventeenth centuries, science developed rapidly within the Western world. The dominant religion, Christianity, embraced all five of the presuppositions mentioned earlier under *The Basis of Science*.

The Bible stressed that nature was not God, but the creation of God. By contrast, the ancient Greeks believed the earth was a semi-divine creature. This hindered experimental work. For if nature was like a divine being, then performing experiments on 'her' seemed rather like committing sacrilege. But in Christianity nature was demoted from being an object of worship. It was untamed and needed to be subdued, though 'subdue' did not mean 'exploit'. People were to be responsible managers. They were not the owners. But since you could not subdue what you did not understand, there appeared to be a strong encouragement to do science.

Also, since God is a free agent, experiments needed to be carried out to find out the way the world *is*, as distinct from the way we might think it *ought* to be.

John Ray, a seventeenth-century naturalist, referred to science as 'a fit subject for a Sabbath day's study'. James Clerk Maxwell, a nineteenth-century mathematician and physicist, placed what has been called the 'research workers' text' above the door of the Cavendish laboratory in Cambridge. This text from Psalm 111, 'The works of the Lord are great, sought out of all them that have pleasure therein', also finds a place over the entrance to the new Cavendish laboratory.

Philosophers and historians have pointed to the prevailing Christian belief in a rational, orderly God as providing fertile soil for the growth of experimental science.

"Teach us to study the works of Thy hands that we may subdue the earth to our use, and strengthen our reason for Thy service."

James Clerk Maxwell

THE SEARCH FOR INDEPENDENCE

The partnership of Christianity with science was commonly accepted until the last decades of the nineteenth century. A lot of clergymen were scientists, and their understanding of the world deepened their faith rather than destroyed it.

The nineteenth century brought changes. It was not simply that new scientific discoveries (evolution, for example, and the age of the earth) raised questions about Christian beliefs. It was because the new breed of professional scientists wanted to conduct their science without reference to the church. Up until then the church was the dominant voice in society. But with the industrial revolution, many scientists began to see their role as central and science as offering more important knowledge.

Behind the science and religion debates of the nineteenth century was a struggle for independence:

■ **Many scientists wanted their experiments and theories to be *intellectually* independent of religion. They didn't want to talk about God's design of the world, only of causes leading to effects.**

■ **Many scientists wanted their own role in society to be *culturally* independent of the church. The church was no longer to be the all-powerful source of knowledge.**

THE 'X-CLUB'

In some cases the portrayal of science and religion as enemies has been deliberate. For example, a group of nine famous Victorian scientists, eight of whom were Fellows of the Royal Society, banded together into a group called the 'X-Club'. The group shared an anti-clerical attitude, declaring that 'the bond that united us was devotion to science, pure and free, untrammelled by religious dogmas'.

Professor Colin Russell has described it in this way:

'The movement spawned by the X-Club and its sympathizers has been called "Victorian scientific naturalism". In its simplest form this was a concerted attempt to replace conventional religion (which deals with the supernatural) by a world-view that involves nature and nature only. Its aim was the secularization of society. There were two distinct aspects, or phases, of the strategy adopted. First of all the church (that is, the Established Church) had to be discredited . . . Three centuries of alliance between Christianity and science were quickly forgotten and a new mythology engineered . . . In attacking the church, "Mother Nature" was an indispensable ally. She was, in short, a substitute for God . . . The second phase of the strategy was not so much to *attack* the church as to *imitate* it. Thomas Huxley spoke of the "new Reformation" heralded by modern science. He preached "lay sermons" on scientific subjects, spoke of his colleagues as "the church scientific" and of himself as its "bishop" . . . At some lectures a hymn to creation was sung by the respectful "congregation".'

From the time of the nineteenth-century industrial revolution, science has been thought of as the most important area of knowledge.

The campaign was remarkably successful and its effects are still seen in a widespread belief that science and religion are at war.

Commenting on the 'warfare model', Professor Russell adds,

'A whole new literature emerged as "history" was rewritten, literature that today is almost universally regarded as worthless for any true insights into the close historical interactions between religion and science. The depths were probably reached with J.W.Draper's *History of the Conflict between Religion and Science* of 1875 and A.D.White's *A History of the Warfare of Science with Theology in Christendom* of 1895. There were dozens of lesser works telling the same story and scholars are still having to live with an enduring mythology which has etched itself deeply into the national consciousness, precisely as intended.'

The 'conflict thesis' is a simplistic view of a complex area of study. Some tensions have undoubtedly arisen through failing to recognize the limitations as well as the strengths of science and it is to these that we now turn.

THE LIMITATIONS OF SCIENCE

Which of the following questions can be answered by science, and which cannot?

- How are atomic bombs made?
- Should we make atomic bombs?
- How did the universe begin?
- Did God create the universe?
- How does a compact disc work?
- Is playing a compact disc enjoyable?

Despite abuses which sometimes give science a bad name, it is a success story. It enables the understanding and prediction of events in the physical world and their control through technology. Had science not been so successful, it would probably never have been imagined to be the final court of appeal for judging all other kinds of knowledge.

But you cannot measure the beauty of a sunset with a multimeter. Neither is it any use asking science to show whether there is a God. Science is the study of the physical world. Questions about God's existence are outside its terms of reference.

Religious behaviour can, of course, be studied scientifically. It is a part of human behaviour which can be observed and described. But this is quite different from saying that science can tell us about God.

The limitations of science are not so much in the *territory it explores*, for every physical object or event is in principle open to scientific study. They lie rather in the *methods it uses*, the questions it can answer and the types of explanations it gives.

Science cannot tell us whether courses of action—including scientific experiments—are right or wrong, only what the likely consequences will be. A seventeenth-century scientist, Robert Boyle, refused to make known some of his discoveries about invisible inks. He was afraid they would be used for mischievous purposes.

MECHANISM AND MEANING

Science is concerned with the *mechanisms* of our world whereas religion is concerned with the *meaning* of life. The distinction between the two can be illustrated by looking at two different but compatible meanings to the question 'Why am I alive?'

■ **mechanism**
Why am I alive? 'What physical processes, from the very first atoms and molecules, led to my being alive?'

■ **meaning**
Why am I alive? 'Is there any ultimate purpose for my being me?'

Science and religion are largely concerned with different questions. A danger appears when science is viewed as the final court of appeal about *any* kind of knowledge. In the early part of this century such a view became fashionable and seems to have become firmly entrenched in popular thinking and the media.

Mechanism

Why am I alive?

What keeps the blood flowing round my body?

How do my cells divide and replicate?

Meaning

Why am I alive?

Was I created by God?

Is there a purpose to creation, or is it a gigantic accident?

Is there any ultimate purpose for my being me?

LOGICAL POSITIVISM

The belief that science is the final court of appeal about any claims to knowledge came from a view of science called 'positivism', so named from the belief that science gave 'certain' or 'positive' knowledge through the senses. In the 1920s it was developed by a group of philosophers called the Vienna Circle. They made it into a full-blown theory about what could, and what could not, be meaningfully said about anything. The theory went under the name of *logical* positivism, so-called because its ideas were believed to follow as a matter of logic from the positivism of science.

Logical positivism dismissed religious talk as meaningless. It left the impression that science, and science alone, proves things, and that anything, like religion, which cannot be 'proved scientifically' is not worth accepting.

If it *were* true that science could lead us into all truth, then since science can only tell us about material things, it would necessarily follow that material things were all there were! Talk of the spiritual world would be meaningless.

Some people, who imagined that science

was like this, made impossible demands like 'prove to me scientifically that God exists'. When this could not be done, they concluded that science had displaced God.

"Scientists are no more irreligious than other people. But the nature of their work concentrates their attention on questions of *mechanism*, and this very concentration tends to put out of focus questions of *meaning*."
Professor Douglas Spanner

But does this popular picture of science as *the* supreme example of knowledge stand up to close inspection? Why, for example, do few philosophers now support it?

One reason for the lack of support is that it turns out to be fatal to science itself, on which the ideas were supposed to have been built! For science involves making assumptions, like the uniformity of nature, which cannot be proved by the experience of our senses alone. So, to say it is meaningless to talk about things which cannot be proved by our senses, undermines science itself.

SCIENTISM

Giving to science the false image of being free from error and the source of all truth is 'Scientism' rather than science. It is the image of science which some advertisers like to promote. And if it is 'new', as well as being 'scientific', that is looked on as even better. But the very use of the word 'new' is a reminder that both the *content* of science changes and so does the *philosophy* of science—views as to what the activity of science is all about. Science is 'unfinished business' and there is no way of being absolutely sure we have arrived at a true understanding.

Most areas of ambiguity in science were, until recently, left out of school science courses. So there is a danger of giving the impression that science is indisputable fact, in contrast to religion, where there often appears to be little agreement.

"It ought not to be overlooked that there are more disagreements and apparent contradictions within science itself than there are between science and religion. Conflict between rival views is quite common in science."

Professor Malcolm Dixon

Advertisers of household-technology products like to give the impression that 'the appliance of science' is bound to bring a better life.

PART THREE: EXPLAINING EXPLANATIONS

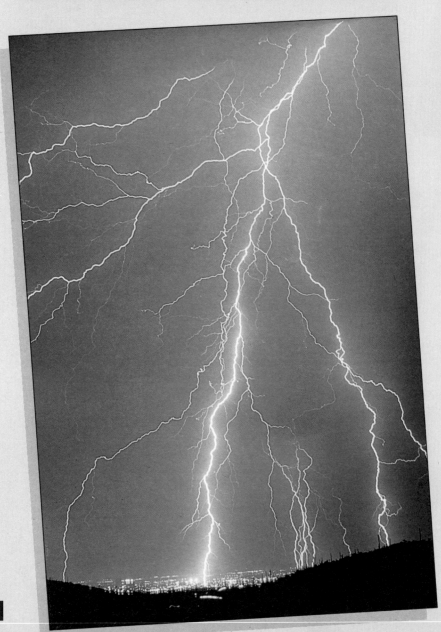

Religious experience is only a psychological neurosis.

Now we understand all about evolution, we don't need the simple stories of Genesis.

The tone of voice and the context would normally give the clues. The words at face value could be answered by saying, 'because energy is transferred, raising the temperature of the water until its vapour pressure is equal to that of the surrounding atmosphere, when it boils.' Or it could be answered 'because I want a cup of tea', getting the reply 'I know that; that wasn't what I was asking. I want an explanation of why you're flouting rules which forbid eating and drinking in laboratories.'

Since science and religion concern themselves with different types of explanations, this sets boundaries to where we can sensibly turn for answers to questions about the world we live in.

For physical explanations of how it began we go to physics and chemistry. For explanations of the development of living matter we turn to biology. But for explanations of ultimate purpose in the universe, we look to science in vain.

Scientific explanations try to show that single events, like the falling of a particular object, fit in with general patterns which are true for all objects everywhere. These general patterns are described in *scientific laws*—in this case, the law of gravity.

Science appears to explain many religious phenomena. Scientists seem to have all the answers. Ancient tribal people may have thought of thunder and lightning as the voice of God; we know it as electrical discharges in the atmosphere.

To explain means to make plain. There are many different ways of making something plain, so there are many different types of explanation. This sometimes causes confusion!

Imagine a kettle of water boiling in the corner of a laboratory. The person in charge of the laboratory sees the kettle and asks the student, 'Why is that kettle of water boiling over there?' The question, on paper, is ambiguous.

'Why is that kettle boiling?' There are quite different ways of answering such seemingly simple questions.

TYPES OF EXPLANATION

Different types of explanation can be illustrated by showing how they answer different types of questions about something a little out of the ordinary—a chronometer.

Not all the possible types of explanation are needed every time. A historian would not need a scientific explanation in order to write an account of this piece of maritime history. Nor would a scientist need to mention John Harrison, the inventor. This does not make each other's explanations invalid; it just reflects their narrowly defined subject interests. The types of explanation are not logically in *competition* with each other, but *compatible*.

By compatible we mean they are capable of existing together without discord or disharmony: the two views are consistent.

One of the main misunderstandings about explanations in science and in religion is to overlook the fact that reason-giving scientific explanations can exist side-by-side with reason-giving explanations based on motives. The common tendency to think that one type of explanation can oust another of a different type has been compared to one noisy fledgling in a nest trying to evict others which have an equal and independent right to be there. It seems we get mentally frustrated by things we cannot explain. So it may be that *any* type of explanation relieves the sense of frustration, so that other types are not sought and may even be denied.

HARRISON'S CHRONOMETER

Interpretative explanation

Q What is it?

A An instrument for telling the time very accurately, a special kind of clock.

Descriptive explanation

Q How is it constructed?

A From cog wheels, springs, pivots, hands and a balance wheel.

Reason-giving (scientific) explanation

Q Why does it keep time so accurately?

A The expansion of a lever with changing temperature causes a compensating change in the length of the hairspring.

Reason-giving (motives) explanation

Q Why was it invented?

A To determine longitude accurately at sea in order to save sailors' lives and time.

FIRST THINGS FIRST

Isaac Newton (1642–1727) is famous for his theory of gravity. In a letter to a friend, he said 'the Rotations of the Planets could not be derived from Gravity, but required a divine Arm to impress them'. What did Newton mean?

In scientific writings of those times it was common to talk about both 'First Causes' and 'Secondary Causes'. Secondary Causes were the physical causes studied in science. 'There was a Big Bang' would be a modern Secondary Cause explanation for the existence of the universe. 'God brought the universe into being' would be a 'First Cause' explanation.

Nowadays, science limits itself to Secondary Causes. This does not mean that modern scientists do not believe in God—some do and some

Isaac Newton regarded his theological writings as more important than his scientific ones.

do not. Nor do the lack of references to God in scientific papers mean that science has displaced God: you can study the science involved in a television set without mentioning the inventor of television.

An event is said to be scientifically explained if, knowing the relevant laws and what things were like beforehand, the event was to be expected. With the origins of our universe, however, there is no 'beforehand' and it seems unlikely that the ordinary laws of physics held under the kinds of conditions which existed in the first fraction of a second of the Big Bang.

However far scientists probe towards the beginning of the universe, a creator cannot be either proved or disproved by the results.

Despite the practical difficulties of studying such a unique event, scientists look for physical answers to physical questions. God is not suddenly encountered at the end of the line. If you uncover the secret of a micro-circuit on a chip using a powerful microscope, you do not suddenly come across its maker as you sort out the last piece of circuitry. But certain popularizers of science imply similar things when they claim that complete scientific explanations of the origins of the universe rule out a Maker:

"That such a universe as ours did emerge with exactly the right blend of forces may have the flavour of a miracle, and therefore seem to require some form of intervention [by God]. But nothing intrinsically lacks an explanation. We cannot yet see quite far enough to decide which is the right explanation, but we can be confident that intervention [by God] was not necessary."
Dr Peter Atkins

DOES SCIENCE NEED GOD?

We do not always make use of all the different types of explanation there are.

In concentrating on one aspect of an event, we may only *need* explanations of one type to build up a consistent picture. A detective concentrating on the motive for a murder may be preoccupied with explanations of why the crime was committed. A pathologist, on the other hand, may be engrossed with explanations of the physical factors which caused the victim's heart to stop beating. In this sense the pathologist has no 'need' of explanations of why the murder was committed in order to

do his or her job. But it would be nonsense to say that explanations of the murderer's plan and purpose could be denied on this account.

It is only in this restricted sense of the word 'need' that it is correct to say, 'there is no need to invoke the idea of a Supreme Being' in order to do science. A scientist can investigate the world of physical cause and effect, without once referring to God. But as soon as scientists begin to ask why there is a universe to study, or why nature operates in a regular, uniform way, or whether or not there is a mind behind the laws they observe, they are looking for different types of

explanations from scientific ones.

The claim that physical explanations of the origins of the universe make it impossible to believe in a creator makes a similar mistake to the claim that physical explanations of an invention makes it impossible to believe in an inventor.

The task of science is to give explanations, but it can only provide certain types.

■ **Physics and chemistry** explain what our bodies are made up of—their atoms and molecules.

■ **Biology** explains how our bodies work—digestion, movement and reproduction.

■ **Psychology** explains our behaviour—how we learn, how changes in belief take place.

■ **Sociology** explains how we behave in a society—what it is that influences the behaviour of groups of people.

Scientific explanations are not the only types there are, nor are they necessarily the best ones. If the task is to make a medicine to kill off certain bacteria, then a scientific explanation of the patient's body chemistry is best for finding the necessary medical knowledge. But if the knowledge required is of a personal kind, aimed at striking up a friendship, then the atom-and-molecule explanation of the person is inappropriate.

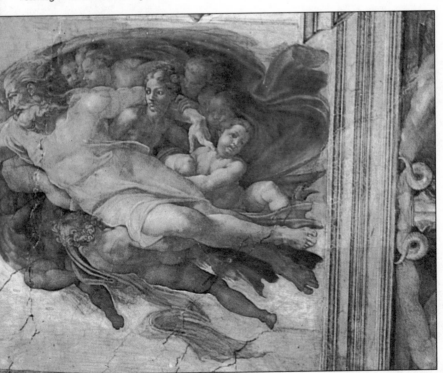

PUSHING GOD OUT

Many years ago, some theologians thought God was getting pushed out because scientific writers were talking more about physical cause-and-effect and less about God. But there is nothing sinister about this.

It is perfectly acceptable to take science as the study of the physical world and to discuss questions about God in a separate subject called theology, or 'God-talk'. There is no necessary contradiction in believing *both* that it is God's doing *and* that there are physical explanations for how it happens. But in the past some said, 'We thought it was God who kept the planets in their orbits, but the scientists tell us it's gravity'. So they looked around for unexplained gaps in the knowledge of the natural world and said, 'Ah, the scientists don't understand that—so that must be God'.

On this view, as the mechanisms of the universe became better understood, God's part inevitably got smaller.

'God-of-the-gaps' thinking confuses different types of explanation. It tries to plug up the gaps in scientific explanations with religious ones.

Religious people who believe in a 'god-of-the-gaps' also take the view that certain areas are fenced off to science *because* they are God's working. It comes in expressions such as, 'If life comes from God, scientists will never be able to discover how it arises.' But this does not follow.

Some atheists have confused different types of explanations in the same way as these theologians. But whereas the *theologians* looked for what *had not* been explained (to find a

place for God), the atheists drew attention to what *had* been explained (so as to try to displace God!). One has recently said that since we are so much nearer to understanding the universe's beginning, 'there is no *need* to invoke the idea of a Supreme Being'.

"When we come to the scientifically unknown, our correct policy is not to rejoice because we have found God; it is to become better scientists."
Professor Charles Coulson

GOD OF THE GAPS

As each scientific discovery narrowed the gaps in our knowledge of the world, some Christians tended to define the area of God's work more narrowly, restricting it to what was currently unexplained by science. This mistaken approach ends in God being squeezed out.

The whole world is the result of God working.

Scientists can change living things by genetic engineering. Maybe, but they will never be able to make things live.

Stars were made by hydrogen collecting under gravity. All right, but God must have made the hydrogen.

Amino-acids (the building blocks of life) have been constructed in a laboratory from simple chemicals. OK, but God set up the initial conditions.

Scientists trace the origins of the universe to a Big Bang. But they won't understand how the Big Bang itself started. God did that.

3 NOTHING BUT . . . ?

If a girl said to her boyfriend, 'I love you, even though you're nothing but

■enough phosphorus to make two thousand matches

■enough iron to make a medium sized nail

■enough chlorine to disinfect a swimming pool

■and enough fat for ten bars of soap

. . . she would probably find herself looking for a new boyfriend. To say that an explanation of the chemical make-up of a person is *all* there is to be said about them is a gross insult. But why? It is not that the explanation is wrong. We *are* made up of chemicals like carbon, oxygen, nitrogen, sulphur and phosphorus,

NOTHING BUTTERY

"Humans are collections of chemicals"

"Humans are *nothing but* collections of chemicals"

The way the first statement changed by adding the two words 'nothing but' may be clearer after looking at a parallel example:

"Sentences are collections of letters of the alphabet"

"Sentences are *nothing but* collections of letters of the alphabet"

What about the collection below?

aabde ee e hhiiiknnn oooop rsssst uuy

Clearly there is a difference between this and the same collection set out as below:

there is a poisonous snake behind you

It is only true to say that 'sentences are nothing but collections of letters of the alphabet' in the sense that if you take all the letters of the alphabet away, one by one, there would be nothing left over. But it would be misleading to imply that a list of the letters says everything, even if the list is given in the right order. For a new property has emerged which is not part of the ordered list of letters—the *meaning* of the sentence. It speaks of a threat and requires instant action.

Similarly, it is true that 'humans are nothing but collections of chemicals', only in the restricted sense that if you took all the chemicals away, nothing would be left.

which would only cost a few dollars if purchased separately. The danger, and the error, lies in those two words, *nothing but*. Yes, we *are* chemicals, but we are far from being *nothing but chemicals.*

Take the collection of chemicals that is you. The element sulphur is yellow. The element carbon comes in two forms, diamond and graphite. The latter is black. Going down the scale of size you could say you are made up of atoms of sulphur, atoms of carbon, and so forth.

Going still farther down the scale of size, all these chemicals can be explained as collections of particles, such as neutrons, protons and electrons. So are we *nothing but* (those words again) a collection of sub-atomic particles?

Does this process of reducing everything to smaller and smaller size stop. Or is the world like a set of Russian dolls?

2 + 2 = ?

It is neat and tidy to be able to express everything in the universe in terms of about a hundred basic building-bricks, or elements, each made up of a smaller range of 'elementary' particles.

But the price to be paid for continually reducing in a search for simplicity can be to lose sight of the importance of the way the basic 'building bricks' are arranged. The order gives rise to properties which the 'building bricks' themselves do not have.

If hydrogen and oxygen are *mixed* together, we are left with gases. But if they *combine* together, they form a more complex substance—water—and a new property emerges because of their combination. The *emergent* property is 'wetness', which is not possessed by the atoms of the gases themselves.

Again, all atoms of carbon are alike but if they are joined one way, graphite is formed; if they are joined differently, diamond is the result.

Then again, colour is a property of

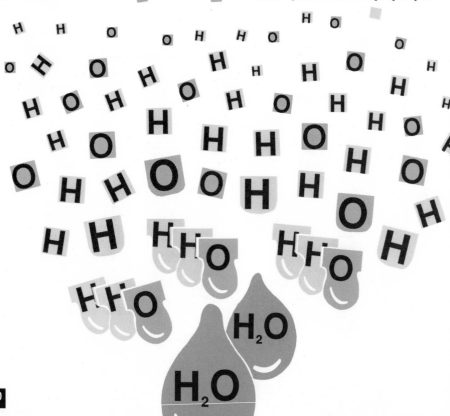

the element sulphur, but colour is not a property of the protons, neutrons and electrons that make it up. The property of colour only emerges because of the way the elementary particles are linked up into a large collection of atoms.

When elements combine they form compounds. Carbon is rather special in forming an enormous number of important compounds and these compounds can be so complicated that a new property may emerge—the ability for the chemicals to *replicate*, to make copies of the compounds

themselves. At this stage the border is crossed between living and non-living things.

Living things may be very simple forms of life, like the amoeba, or vastly more complex creatures like ourselves. Consciousness is another example of an emergent property. Only above certain levels of complexity do we find conscious thought and self-awareness.

LEVELS OF EXPLANATION

The same individual being can be 'explained' at different levels:
■ the level of protons, neutrons and electrons
■ the level of atoms and molecules
■ the level of cells
■ the level of persons

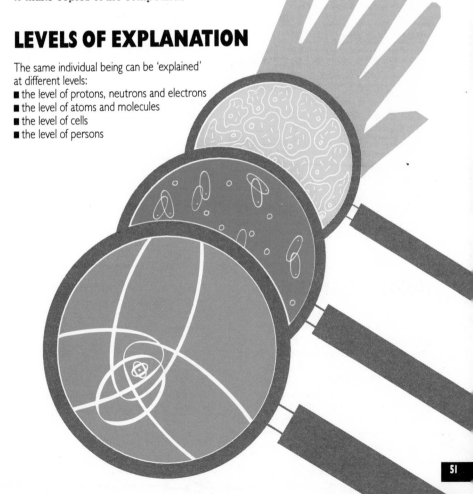

EXPLAINING AWAY?

It is easy to imagine that scientific explanations 'explain away' any purpose for which we are here or for which the universe was made. This is why some religious people find explanations of religious experiences threatening. Some who do not believe in a God behind the experience will see such explanations as debunking the experience itself. They may use expressions such as, 'It's all psychological'.

But human behaviour is open to scientific explanation. Psychologists and sociologists study human behaviour, and religious experience is part of that behaviour.

So how might a psychologist, acting in a professional capacity, explain religious experience? (It should not, of course, be assumed that the psychologist is irreligious; some are, others are themselves religious believers.)

Typically, they would talk in terms of a *stimulus* arousing us, our *response* being the action we take, and the *reinforcement* as that which encourages us to continue with our beliefs and actions.

On the other hand, a Christian would be more likely to refer to the action of God in his or her life, using words like *repentance* (change of mind), *conversion* (change of direction), *regeneration* (new birth) and the work of the Holy Spirit.

The issue of truth is the key one.
Are the religious beliefs true or not? Obviously if drugs are used as a stimulus to change people's beliefs, psychiatric explanations might be able to 'explain away' either the appearance or the disappearance of beliefs.

Where the beliefs are true, the various types of explanations can be valid and complete in their own terms. They neither 'need', nor contradict each other. A psychological explanation of change in belief does

REDUCTIONISM

There is nothing wrong with reducing explanations to the atom and molecule level as a technique in science, only in claiming this is *all* there is to be said. This is called 'reductionism' because it reduces everything to its component parts. It is also called 'Nothing-buttery', since 'nothing but' acts like a red light to warn about a reductionist claim: for example, we are *nothing but* a collection of atoms. Other warning words are 'only', 'just' and 'simply'.

Reductionism arises in some criticisms of religious beliefs. For example, to deny that human beings have a spiritual nature *because* they are made up solely of atoms and molecules is reductionistic. It simply does not follow. The Book of Genesis recognizes the ordinary nature of what we are made of when it says, 'dust you are and to dust you will return'. It also refers to the grandeur of this organized collection of atoms and molecules as made 'in the image of God'.

not explain away a religious one. 'Explaining' is not the same thing as 'explaining away'. Nor does naming a religious experience as 'psychological' help to explain what has happened. For naming is not the same thing as explaining. And to call religious experience psychological 'explains' nothing. It simply reminds us of what we already knew, that religious practice is one sort of human behaviour.

Sociologists, like psychologists, look for explanations of the ways humans behave. Their area of study is the way we act in groups or in society. They may look, for example, at the function that religion plays in a social group (perhaps it is being used to justify the actions of powerful or wealthy groups in society), and what encourages the growth or decline of religious beliefs within a society.

But one significant factor is missing from such explanations. None of them refer to the truth, or otherwise, of what is believed. Psychological and sociological explanations typically try to explain the *origins* of belief without examining their claim to be true. They ignore questions of ultimate truth. Their concerns are with the *causes* of belief rather than with the *grounds* for judging them to be true or false.

As a method of working, there is nothing wrong with this so long as two points are kept constantly in mind:

■ **These are partial ways of looking at human behaviour.**

■ **They do not rule out the importance of facing up to the issue of the truth or falsehood of the beliefs.**

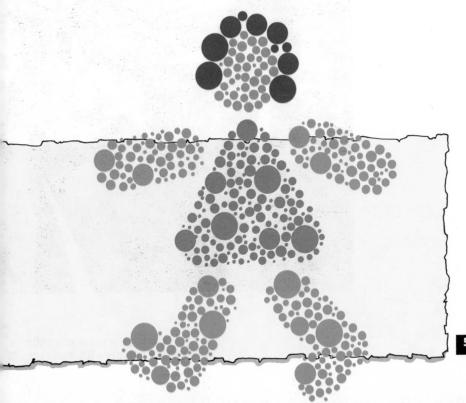

PART FOUR: BELIEF AND EVIDENCE

Everyone has beliefs of some kind.

How do we know what to believe?
How do we use evidence to decide
what is true?

■ There is no God

■ There is life
on other planets

■ Doing the same scientific
experiment gives the same results

■ The world is real and not a dream
■ We have missed the last train
■ Performing a particular dance will make it rain

FINDING THE TRUTH

'TRUE FOR YOU'

The matter of 'truth' is a difficult topic. Relativists deny that any one belief is more true than another. The meaning of 'truth' is changed from 'what is believed corresponds in some ways to things as they actually are' to 'meaningful', or 'true for you'. This implies it may not be 'true' for someone else. Beliefs are regarded simply as the products of the believer's upbringing or culture.

Certainly, beliefs are powerfully affected by culture. But that is very different from denying their truth or falsity. A person born in an Islamic country may grow up a Muslim. Someone whose parents never believed in God may readily adopt the same views. But the key question is not the majority opinion or the cultural pressures to conform. It is: are there adequate grounds for holding a belief to be true?

Relativism, by denying absolute truth, also runs into the problem of reflexivity—it trips itself up. For if there are no absolute truths about matters of belief, what about the central belief of relativism that 'there are no absolutes truths; all is relative'? Is this true or not? If it is true, relativism is false, because at least one thing—its central belief—is true! If it is false, it forfeits its claim to be accepted.

When thinking about beliefs, it is important to distinguish between the causes for belief, and the grounds—or evidence—for belief itself. It is to this distinction that we now turn.

Focus
Grounds for belief.

Method
Philosophers and historians examine the claim that God exists and has spoken to us.

Question
Are the beliefs true?

CONTENT, CAUSES AND GROUNDS

Question
What beliefs do people hold?

Method
Researchers conduct surveys and study world religions.

Focus
Content of belief.

Focus
Causes of belief.

Method
Sociologists and anthropologists investigate the factors which encourage or discourage people in holding religious beliefs.

Question
What causes people to hold religious beliefs?

4 CAUSES AND GROUNDS

On the previous page we raised this question of the difference between causes and grounds. It needs spelling out in more detail.

■ **Causes of belief** may include subjective factors like fear, wishful thinking and need of security. They may include family upbringing. There is nothing wrong about wanting security and hoping for better things — or even feeling fear, if there is something which needs to be avoided for our good. The motive for accepting or rejecting a belief does not invalidate it.

Neither is it a bad thing for our own beliefs to be affected by those we were brought up with, provide we resist two extremes. One is to take these beliefs on board as a 'packaged deal' without thinking them through. The other is to reject them simply to be different. Neither of these are adequate foundations for a set of beliefs for life. Unexamined beliefs are less likely to stand the test of time.

Causes, such as family upbringing, do not in themselves say anything about whether a belief is true or not.

To imagine a set of beliefs is explained away simply by describing their historical origins is to fall into the 'genetic fallacy' (from *genesis* meaning 'origins'). It is also to wield a double-edged sword for, as the adjacent story shows, if it *were* an argument, it would be as damaging to the sceptic as to the believer.

■ **Grounds for belief** are objective factors which exist independently of whether anyone believes them or not.

The distinction between causes

and grounds can be illustrated from the following beliefs. In each case there is a *cause* for the belief, signalled by the word '*because*'. But there are only *grounds* for some of them:

1. Susan believed she had won the draw because her ticket had her lucky number on it.

2. Susan believed she had won the draw because someone said they had seen her name on the list of prize winners.

3. Susan believed she had won the draw because she had seen her name on the official list of prize winners.

Suppose the person who told Susan they had seen her name on the list was lying. They had not even seen the list. But it was still true that Susan's name *was* on the list and that she *had* won. So Susan would be believing the right thing for the wrong reason.

But she would not have been *justified* in believing it, even though it was true. Only in the last instance would there have been *grounds* for believing she had won. In that case we would say, 'Susan *knew* she had won the draw', rather than 'Susan *believed* she had won the draw'.

The word 'know' is kept for what is true. Of course there are always questions which can be raised, such as 'was there somebody else with the same first name and surname?' But although we can *believe* things which

may be true *or* false, we can only *know* things that are true. In everyday speech we say we 'know' something if we are sure about it. If we find we have been wrong, we can still say 'I believed it, but I was wrong'; but we cannot say 'I knew it, but I was wrong'.

Some philosophers define knowledge as 'justified, true belief'.

Whether a belief is justified or not depends on the evidence for it.

When can a person rightly say, 'I know I won the lottery'?

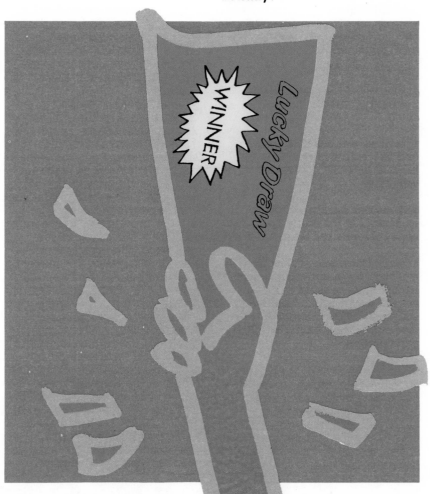

PROOF

Imagine you are trying to catch the last train but believe you have missed it. This belief could be justified by the *direct* evidence of our senses—'I saw it go'. If someone asks, 'Are you sure that was the last train?' we might reply, 'It's past its departure time and this is its usual platform'. But platform alterations occur and trains do make late starts. But if the porter said it *was* our train, we might say, 'It's no use arguing, I *know* I've missed the last train'. But porters can make mistakes. However, with the prospect of a long walk home, we might be irritable with anyone who made that suggestion.

The story makes a number of points:

■ **Justified, true belief depends on external, objective evidence—the *grounds* for belief. It is not simply subjective.**

■ **Sometimes we rely on *indirect* evidence, like the station clock, the empty platform and the signal at red.**

■ **None of those pieces of indirect evidence, *taken separately*, might totally convince us the train had gone. It might, as in a detective story, only be the *cumulative* evidence of many small clues that persuaded us.**

It is not realistic to demand knock-down proofs for everything. We cannot live like that. In science, people once spoke freely about 'proof', meaning 'to show beyond doubt'. Disproving can be easy. Proving beyond all doubt is virtually impossible (except in logic and some branches of mathematics). A scientific law cannot be 'proved' to hold good in *every* untried experiment.

To put it another way, one cannot argue from particular examples, such as 'these swans are white', to the universal statement, 'all swans are white'. One Australian black swan will falsify it.

In every area of life, not only in science, we have to be satisfied with grounds for belief which fall short of absolute certainty. This is why the demand 'prove to me God exists' is unrealistic, if it means 'demonstrate in a way nobody could possibly question'.

Because science does not prove (or verify) things up to the hilt, some philosophers of science think the task of science is to try to *disprove* (or falsify). You set up a hypothesis and then try to knock it down. If you don't succeed, you keep using it for the time being. But care is needed, even with this view. For it is unusual for a theory to be overthrown by one experiment. Mistakes might have been made in the experiment or the results misinterpreted. The rejection of a theory usually waits for a better one to take its place. Thomas Kuhn has described how crises in 'normal science' lead to 'extraordinary science' and 'scientific revolutions' from which new theories emerge.

In religion, there are important differences from the use of evidence in science. For example, evidence for God is not the same as evidence for electrons, although the evidence for both is 'indirect'. Indirect evidence in science is for invisible physical 'objects' like electrons; but God, though invisible, is not a physical object.

'I have missed the last train . . . at least, I think I have . . . ' How can we know things for sure?

Claims about the truth of religious beliefs may make appeals to evidence drawn from religious experience, from history, from looking at the natural world, from reason or from what God makes known to us (his 'revelation').

Some tests for religious truth apply to other disciplines too. For instance, one can ask whether the belief system is **consistent**—free from contradictions. Again, does it hold together and make sense overall—is it **coherent**? Also, does it cover the whole range of human experience—is it **comprehensive**?

Dismissive comments—'it's all a matter of interpretation'—might suggest that religious belief is all a matter of personal preference. But not all interpretations are equally valid. Some interpretations fit the data better than others, whether we like it or not.

It would be misleading to imagine that everyone looking at the same evidence comes to the same conclusion. Sometimes 'the search for truth' is prized more highly than the finding of answers. Seeking costs little; finding could demand an unwelcome change of lifestyle.

"There comes a moment when the children who have been playing at burglars hush suddenly: was that a real footstep in the hall? There comes a moment when people who have been dabbling in religion ('Man's search for God'!) suddenly draw back. Supposing we really found him? We never meant it to come to that! Worse still, supposing he had found us?"

Professor C.S.Lewis

A MATTER OF FAITH

Religious faith has been variously described as 'believing what you know isn't true' and 'an illogical belief in the occurrence of the improbable'. One popular view of the relation between faith and evidence is apparent in the comment, 'Don't confuse me with facts . . . my faith is made up'!

The idea of a contrast between facts and faith is fraught with difficulties. So-called 'facts' involve elements of belief, while beliefs are not simply matters of personal preference but appeal to evidence which is external to the individual.

'Credulity' is a word reserved for the sort of 'faith' which takes no account of facts. 'Credulity' means being too ready to believe, when there is insufficient or contrary evidence.

The difference between credulity and well-grounded faith lies in the weight of the evidence. The supporting evidence for faith can vary enormously as can be seen by listing some things one can have faith in:

Faith can be in a friend, a lucky star, a medicine, a husband or wife. It can be in a surgeon, God or a newspaper report.

Faith can be well-founded or it can be misplaced, but faith is always *in* something. Faith is *not* a word that can stand alone; it must be linked with an object. And it is the *object* of the faith, rather than the *sincerity* of the faith, that is important. Sincerity is a good thing, but it is possible to be sincerely wrong. Sincerely believing a bottle contains healing medicine will be of no help if a bottle of poison is taken off the shelf by mistake.

Religious faith must be grounded in facts if it is to have any final reality. Christians may talk of sensing the presence of God—but they could be deceiving themselves. In the end the Christian faith is based on the evidence of history. Did Jesus live? What did he teach? And, more important, did he rise from the dead as the Bible claims?

Faith involves **belief plus action**. Used in a religious sense, it is similar to trust in a person. It includes the belief that something is true, but it usually goes beyond that into a commitment to actions based on the belief.

"If I have faith, it means that I have decided to do something and am willing to stake my life on it. When Columbus started on his first voyage into the West, he believed that the earth was round and small enough to be circumnavigated. He did not think that this was right in theory alone, but he staked his whole existence on it."

Werner Heisenberg, known best for his Principle of Indeterminacy in physics

Other sea-captains had access to the same slim evidence that was available to Columbus. But they did not set sail and so never discovered a New World.

In the Bible, faith means more than believing God exists or that he created the world. When people have 'faith' it means they trust God for forgiveness and for help to live as God asks. It means committed action, not simply believing.

COMMON SENSE

While this can help to avoid credulity, it can mislead. As its name *common* sense implies, it judges what is believable on the basis of past experience. So if something novel comes along which seems incredible on that basis, it may get rejected, even if true.

In the sixteenth century, it offended common sense to suppose that the earth could be rushing through space.

At the start of this century, it was contrary to common sense to think that so-called 'solid matter' is mainly space, but now we accept it. Einstein's theory of relativity, too, is a classic example of how badly common sense can mislead.

It is easy to dismiss any religious claims which appear to contradict common sense, but caution is needed. Common sense is not an infallible guide to truth.

No one begins a rock climb without believing they can do it. But belief on its own is not enough; the climber has to start going up the cliff.

PART FIVE: MIRACLES

It was a miracle she climbed out of the wreckage alive.

His parachute didn't open. It's a miracle he's alive to tell the tale.

It was nothing short of a miracle that I passed that exam.

They prayed for her and she was healed—it's a miracle!

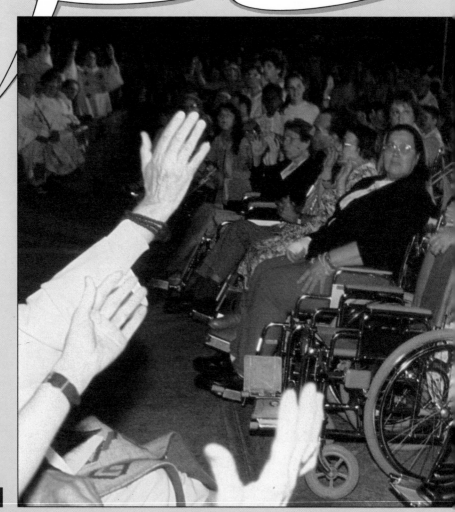

These uses of the word 'miracle' show how widely the word is used to express wonder and amazement. When it is used in a religious sense, it often takes the extra meaning of being a sign from God.

A common view of miracle is an event which 'breaks' the laws of nature. But is this view adequate?

The central miracle in the Bible is the claim that Jesus rose from the dead. But everyday science and medical experience say dead people do not rise again. They may be resuscitated from near death, they may recover from coma, but they do not come back to life after many hours of death.

So, can we believe in miracles? Or are they the outdated expressions of a credulous and superstitious age? And if we discover any natural causes for what we once regarded as a miracle, does the 'miracle' cease to be the work of God?

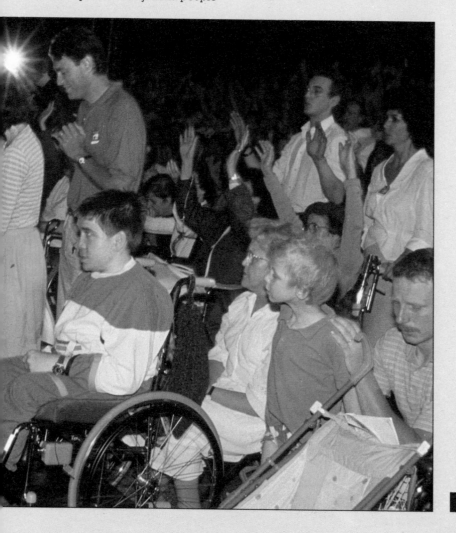

WHAT IS A MIRACLE?

It is difficult to find a neat and tidy answer to this question, even one which fits all the miracles recorded in the Bible.

In Jewish history, the escape from Egypt across the Red Sea is seen as a sign of God's care for his oppressed people.

Earlier in the story Moses went to Pharaoh to demand, in God's name, that the Israelites be released from slavery. Moses was told to show various miracles as signs that the demand came from God. We are told that Pharaoh's magicians were able to duplicate some, but not all, of these miracles. So, not all miracles are claimed to be due to the power of God.

So what is a miracle?

A simple start might be to say that a miracle is 'an act of God which cannot be explained'. But straightaway the definition would fall down over the examples of the crossing of the Red Sea and the feats of Pharaoh's magicians. In the first, the physical mechanism *is* explained—'the Lord caused the sea to go back by a strong east wind all that night', as the writer

of Exodus put it. In the second, the wonders are not attributed to God.

The main characteristics of a miracle are:

■ **Something amazing happens which catches the attention because of its nature, its timing, or both;**

■ **The amazing event is intended by God as a sign.**

Although the Red Sea crossing is an exception, the mechanisms of miracles are not usually explained in the Bible. Although there appears to be no reason why people should not try to guess the *how* of miracles, doing so may divert attention from the *why*—the significance—which is the central point.

MIRACLES IN THE NEW TESTAMENT

Miracle stories were common in New Testament times. But they are also to be found before and since, and occur in other world religions. Well-known New Testament miracles are the feeding of the five thousand, the changing of water into wine and the resurrection of Jesus Christ, foundational to Christianity.

These miracles are presented, not as knock-down proofs of who Jesus is, but as an integral part of his mission and his teaching—as 'signs' from God requiring human responses of faith and obedience. Broadly speaking, miracles can be put into two main groups; nature miracles and miracles of healing.

Those who find difficulty with the idea of miracles do so for a variety of reasons. The one we look at in this book is the belief that scientific laws make miracles impossible.

'BREAKING' SCIENTIFIC LAWS?

"Science says miracles can't happen."

This is a common belief because miracles are said to 'break' scientific laws. But can scientific laws be 'broken'? And what are scientific laws, anyway?

The word 'law' is used in more than one way, and this leads to confusion. The most familiar use is in the 'laws of the land'. Here the laws state what should happen. People should not murder or steal from others. The laws are *prescriptive* because they prescribe what should happen—much as medical prescriptions state what drugs should be used. These laws can be broken, as in the case of homicide or robbery.

The laws of the land can be compared to a plan. An architect's plans are prescriptive, showing what the building *should* be like when it's finished.

Scientific laws are completely different. They are *descriptive* as they describe what normally does happen. Scientific laws can be compared to a map, which describes how the land lies. Like a scientific law, if a map does not agree with what the world is like, the map needs to be altered. Map-making makes a useful comparison to the work of the scientist. For, as the lie of the land determines the shape of the map, so the scientific data determine the form of the law—not the other way round.

Boyle's law says that 'the volume of a fixed mass of gas at constant temperature varies inversely with the pressure'. It is a well known scientific law. But there is nothing fixed and unalterable about scientific laws. If later experiments do not fit in with a law, then it is the *law* that needs to be corrected. At high pressures it turns out that Boyle's law does not hold and a more complicated formula is needed.

"The laws of motion do not set billiard balls moving: they analyse the motion after something else . . . has provided it."
Professor C.S.Lewis

Scientific laws no more make events take place the way they do than a map makes a coastline have its shape. Boyle's law does not make the volume of a gas get smaller. The increased pressure does that.

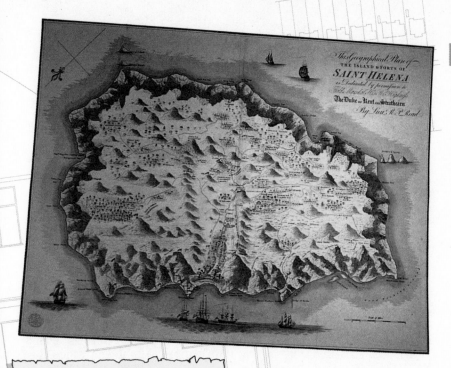

TYPES OF LAW

Laws of the Land

Prescriptive: say what people should do.

Prescribe what ought to take place, as an architect's plans show what should be built.

Laws of the land can be passed by legislatures, and obeyed or ignored.

Scientific Laws

Descriptive: say what does (normally) happen.

Describe what observers see taking place, as a map describes what travellers will find.

Scientific laws cannot be passed, obeyed or broken. They can only be discarded.

The descriptive/prescriptive distinction should not be pressed too far. There is one sense in which scientific laws *do* prescribe something—our *expectations*. On the basis of what has happened before, scientific laws enable us to prescribe (that is, write down beforehand) what is rational to expect.

Scientific laws may indicate what to expect, but they offer no guarantees that things could never be any different. Consequently they say nothing more about the possibility of one-off events like miracles than was known a long time before there was any great interest in science, namely that miracles are not what we would usually expect.

MOTHER NATURE

It would be arrogant to think that people in earlier times were stupid in comparison with us. They knew just as well as we do that it is not natural for virgins to have sons and that it is not natural for people to rise from the dead. The meaning of 'natural' here is what *normally* occurs.

The opposite to 'natural' used in this sense would appear to be 'supernatural'. But there is a difficulty with the word 'supernatural'. For the idea has grown up that, whereas supernatural events are the work of God, natural events take place by themselves. This belief is quite common.

Someone dismissed talk about 'the wonderful flowers God has made', by saying 'It's not God, it's just natural.' This reply contains traces of two different ideas about nature—two ideas which illustrate why a natural/supernatural distinction can be misleading.

One idea is that 'Nature', spelt with a capital 'N', is itself some intelligent organism which 'controls' events. The other idea is that God is not involved in 'natural' events.

During the sixteenth and seventeenth centuries, views of nature underwent a great change. The Greeks had treated nature like a goddess, but now it was seen in a different way. Instead of likening nature to a living organism, it was compared to a vast mechanism. This highlighted the idea of a Maker who was distinct from the creation. The seventeenth-century scientist Robert Boyle understood this from his reading of the Bible. He rejected *pantheism*, which treated God and creation as one and the same. He also disapproved of spelling 'nature' with a capital 'N' and treating it like some goddess—Mother Nature—who could 'plan' and carry things out.

"Having designed the ants, Nature waited for about 150 million years before embarking on her second or human experiment."
Presidential address to the British Association for the Advancement of Science.

It was this kind of talk Boyle opposed. Instead of giving God the credit, nature—the stuff of the world—is treated as though it can think, plan and organize itself. And 'nature' is not the only word treated like this. Other concepts are personified as though they are substitutes for God. Some of them come in the sections on chance and evolution. One which is particularly relevant here is 'laws of nature'.

Laws of nature can be said to be the underlying principles of the universe, which are described as accurately as possible in scientific laws. But sometimes, as was seen in the last section, they get spoken of as though the 'laws' themselves *make* things happen. Charles Kingsley, a friend of Darwin, once said that what we refer to as laws of nature are simply the 'customs of God'. Robert Boyle preferred the term 'rule', because 'law of nature' caused such a lot of confusion.

A COSMIC CLOCKMAKER?

When Robert Boyle made a journey to Strasbourg, he saw a remarkably intricate clock. He compared the relation of the world to God with that of clock to clockmaker.

Just as the clockmaker has designed and made the clock to run in a regular way, so God has created the world to operate in a regular and uniform way. The clockmaker is distinct from the clock, and God is not the universe itself (as the pantheists thought), but the creator of it.

But there is a difficulty. A clock, once wound up, continues to work without further intervention by the clockmaker—until, that is, the mechanism needs rewinding. God, however, is always working in the world, moment by moment. The comparison with the clock breaks down.

In later years, this limitation in the comparison was overlooked. God, like some Cosmic Clockmaker whose work was finished, came to be regarded as having disappeared

The 'deist' philosophers thought of God (the clockmaker) setting in motion the world (the clock). But does this mean he never intervenes again?

from the scene. he had wound up the world—and left. This view of God's activity—or lack of it—is known as *deism*. In its extreme form it virtually amounts to atheism, with God viewed as the Retired Architect or the Absentee Landlord.

The deists believed God had retired from the scene and it was beneath his dignity to interfere with the orderly 'clockwork' of the universe by performing miracles.

Some deists believed God did occasionally 'intervene' in the running of the world to perform the occasional miracle, much as a clockmaker sometimes adjusts the mechanism of his clock.

God was thought of as 'intervening' in the course of nature which was believed normally to function without him. Only events like miracles were called 'supernatural' and regarded as being God at work. Anything which was law-like and 'natural' was not thought to involve God in any day-to-day way after it had first been created. Hence the possible confusion, mentioned earlier, in using words like 'natural' and 'supernatural'.

GOD AT WORK IN THE WORLD

The Bible presents God as the *creator* of the universe. It also portrays him as the *sustainer* of the universe. It is not simply that he was once active, but that he is still active in holding creation in being. Creation is dynamic rather than static.

"(Christ) is the image of the invisible God . . . by him all things were created . . . in him all things hold together."
Paul in his letter to the Colossians

"In these last days God has spoken to us by his Son . . . through whom he made the universe. The Son is the radiance of God's glory and the exact representation of his being, sustaining all things by his powerful word."
The writer to the Hebrews

The idea of a dynamic sustaining needs a very different model to that of a clock. Professor MacKay, a researcher in the mechanisms of the brain, suggested a more contemporary idea of the picture on a TV screen.

"Imagine . . . an artist able to bring his world into being, not by laying down paint on canvas, but by producing an extremely rapid succession of sparks of light on the screen of a television tube. The world he invents is now not static but dynamic, able to change and evolve at his will. Both its form and its law of change (if any) depend on the way in which he orders the sparks of light in

space and time. The scene is steady and unchanging just for as long as he wills it so; but if he were to cease his activity, his invented world would not become chaotic; it would simply cease to be."

Mackay thought of this picture in the 1960s. Today our screens are full of computer-generated graphics. An artist uses computer graphics to generate images, frame by frame. Usually, of course, the pictures are stored and played back time after time. But imagine an artist doing it live! If the artist stopped, then the image, too, would disappear. In a similar way, God can be thought of as sustaining the world second by second.

This view of God as constantly active in creation results in a very different view of miracles from that of 'intervention'. Miracles are not God intervening where he does not usually act, but God acting in different ways from usual.

Miracles are only miracles when they take place within an orderly framework of events. Perhaps the *normal* and the *unusual*, or the *ordinary* and the *extraordinary* acts of God would more closely mirror the Bible's teaching than 'natural' and 'supernatural'.

5

God's creation is dynamic, not static. The creator is involved in every step of his creation.

73

PART SIX: WATCH YOUR LANGUAGE!

People sometimes criticize religion for being 'full of talk about kings, shepherds, judges, light, wind and old men in the sky'. 'Why', they ask, 'cannot religion keep to plain language like science does?'

But just how plain is the 'plain language' of science?

When we want to talk about things which are new, invisible or difficult to understand, we have to resort to 'analogies'—comparisons with familiar things. This applies to science as well as to religion.

IS GOD A FORCE FIELD?

Science uses comparisons.

- The electric current makes the bulb give off light;

- Atoms are thought of as miniature solar systems;

- Light waves bend around corners.

The first and last comparisons are not so obvious as the middle one, but they are there. The word 'current' comes from comparing electricity to a 'flow' or 'current' of water. 'Waves' compares light with water, to help understand why light bends round corners.

Both science and religion resort to *similes*—'God is like a father'; 'the passage of electricity along a wire is *like* a current of water flowing in a pipe'.

Science and religion also use *metaphors*. The word 'like' is dropped, which gives 'God is a father', and 'an electric current is flowing round the circuit'. The words 'current' and 'flowing' have become so familiar that we rarely pause to think where the comparison came from.

"It is a serious mistake to think that metaphor is an optional thing which poets and orators may put into their work as a decoration and plain speakers can do without. The truth is that if we are going to talk at all about things which are not perceived by the senses, we are forced to use language metaphorically."
Professor C.S.Lewis

Some analogies, like the water one, are particularly helpful and have been developed in detail. They are then termed *models*—in our example the 'water circuit model'. But these analogies need to be carefully watched! It is easy to believe the picture holds in every respect.

Analogies are not literal descriptions and, because it is easy to confuse them with the reality they are trying to describe, some people have said they should be avoided.

If comparisons or models are to be helpful they need to be made with familar things. Would a comparison of electricity with water in a pipe be helpful to someone who lived in a part of the world with no piped water supply?

THE 'TAPIOCA TRAP'

'People who recommend it [abandoning analogy completely] have not noticed that when they try to get rid of man-like, or as they are called, 'anthropomorphic', images they merely succeed in substituting images of some other kind. 'I don't believe in a personal God', says one, 'but I do believe in a great spiritual force.' What he has not noticed is that the word 'force' has let in all sorts of images about winds and tides and electricity and gravitation. 'I don't believe in a personal God', says another, 'but I do believe we are all part of one great Being which moves and works through us all'—not noticing that he has merely exchanged the image of a fatherly and royal-looking man for the image of some widely extended gas or fluid. A girl I knew was brought up by 'higher thinking' parents to regard God as a perfect 'substance'; in later life she realised that this had actually led her to think of Him as something like a vast tapioca pudding. (To make matters worse, she disliked tapioca.)'
Professor C.S.Lewis

MODEL-MAKING

■ **Models in science**. A simple
scientific model is the 'planetary, or
solar-system model' of atoms.
Electrons are imagined to go round a
central nucleus like planets round the
sun. It is a handy picture so we can
visualize what we cannot see.

Positive Features

■ The atom is mainly space.
■ Most of the mass is concentrated in the
nucleus.

Negative Features

■ The nucleus does not shine like the sun.
■ The forces are electrical, not gravitational.

■ **Models in religion**. It is not surprising that God-talk (theology) stretches language to its limit. All kinds of models are used to try to convey different aspects of God's character. God is compared to a father, a mother, a lover, a judge, a shepherd, to fire, to light and to a wind—to mention just a few.

The model of God as father is, of course, that of a *good* human father.

Positive Features

■ It is to God that we owe our being.
■ God cares for us and disciplines us.

Negative Features

■ Fathers may eventually be cared for by grown-up children.
■ Some fathers get drunk and abuse their children.

6 TOO SMALL A GOD

A pitfall in the use of models is to hang on to inadequate ones when better ones are available. The 'solar system' model is not helpful for advanced science and more complex ones are needed.

"Hydrogen atoms are not solar systems; it is only useful to think of them as if they were such systems if one remembers all the time that they are not. The price of the employment of models is eternal vigilance."
Professor Braithwaite

Similarly, in religion it is not uncommon for people to hold on to childhood comparisons of God which are quite inadequate. J.B.Phillips' book, *Your God is too small*, pointed out how people tend to grow up mentally in their thinking about science and yet to hold on to 'childish conceptions of God which could not stand up to the winds of real life for five minutes'. These include God as a 'Resident Policeman', a 'Grand Old Man' and a 'Managing Director'.

Often, when science and religion are compared, it is *adult* ideas about science which are compared with *childish* ideas about religion. This is a sure recipe for confusion.

Figurative angels, musical instruments, crowns and garlands—poetic symbols for heaven. The use of symbols and models is common to religion and science.

"There is no need to be worried by facetious people who try to make the Christian hope of "Heaven" ridiculous by saying they do not want "to spend eternity playing harps." The answer to such people is that if they cannot understand books written for grown-ups, they should not talk about them. All the scriptural imagery (harps, crowns, gold, etcetera) is, of course, a merely symbolical attempt to express the inexpressible. Musical instruments are mentioned because for many people (not all) music is the thing known in the present life which most strongly suggests ecstasy and infinity. Crowns are mentioned to suggest the fact that those who are united with God in eternity share His splendour and power and joy. Gold is mentioned to suggest the timelessness of Heaven (gold does not rust) and the preciousness of it. People who take these symbols literally might as well think that when Christ told us to be like doves, He meant that we were to lay eggs."

Professor C.S. Lewis

Models are *literary* devices. They are to be 'taken seriously but not literally. They are partial and provisional ways of imagining what is not observable'.

A DIVINE CLOCK-MAKER

Robert Boyle pictured God as having made the world, much as a clockmaker makes a clock.

There are positive features of this 'divine-clockmaker' model:

■ The universe, like the clock, can be seen as the product of intelligent design.

■ God is separate from his creation, like the clockmaker and the clock. This denies pantheism.

■ The universe, like the clock, shows regular patterns of behaviour.

But there are negative features too:

■ A clock, once made, does not need the clockmaker, except for occasional repairs and winding up. But God is continuously involved in sustaining his creation.

■ A clock cannot respond to its maker as we can respond to God.

PART SEVEN: THE GALILEO AFFAIR

"The fame of this outstanding genius rests mostly on discoveries he never made. Galileo did not invent the telescope; nor the microscope; nor the thermometer; nor the pendulum clock. He did not discover the law of inertia; nor the parallelogram of forces or motions; nor the sun spots. He made no contribution to theoretical astronomy; he did not throw down weights from the leaning tower of Pisa, and did not prove the truth of the Copernican system. He was not tortured by the Inquisition, did not languish in its dungeons, did not say *eppur si muove* ('nevertheless it moves'); and he was not a martyr of science."

Arthur Koestler

What he did was to found the modern science of dynamics, which marks out his greatness.

In the thirteenth century a detailed attempt had been made by a Catholic theologian and philosopher, Thomas Aquinas, to link Greek science with certain Bible texts. Consequently, any attack on Aristotle's physics might be seen as an attack on the Bible. So the Galileo affair, as Dr John Brooke has written, was 'not so much science versus religion as science versus the sanctified science of Aristotle'.

The Galileo affair is a story not only of scientific discovery, but of personal rivalries and power struggles. The same science in the hands of a more diplomatic proponent might have led to a completely different outcome. True, there were discussions on how to interpret the Bible, and struggles over authority within the church, but the theologians were not all against Galileo, nor he against them. The story offers a fascinating insight into how science is affected by spiritual, moral and cultural factors. But first some background is needed about Greek astronomy and about the ideas of Copernicus.

7 CIRCLES UPON CIRCLES

For thirteen hundred years the world-picture of a Greek astronomer, Ptolemy, held sway, with its central earth. It was this picture that Copernicus (1473–1543) challenged.

Ptolemy's world-picture assumed that:

■ **no changes take place in the heavens;**

■ **the heavenly bodies are perfect, without blemish;**

■ **they move in perfect circles with uniform speed around the earth.**

The paths of the 'planets' (from the Greek word 'wanderers') caused considerable problems. They appeared to go forward, stop and go backward before going forward once more. But, by ingenious means,

circular motion could be retained.

A second circle, an epicycle, was added with its centre moving round the main circle. The planet was imagined to rotate round the small circle, while the centre of the small circle moved around the circumference of the large one. The path of the planet, viewed from the earth, then appears to make a series of loops in the sky.

By adjusting the radii of the circles and the speeds of rotations, the movement of each planet could be described. Circles upon circles upon circles could be added until the required accuracy was reached. This meant using some eighty circles in all! It enabled astronomical events such as eclipses to be predicted accurately, so it held the field for about thirteen hundred years.

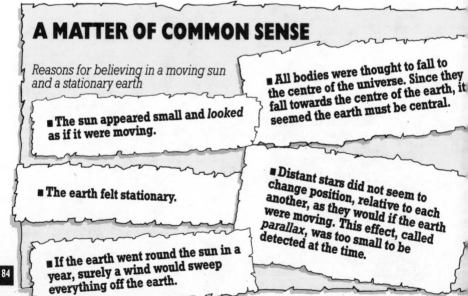

A MATTER OF COMMON SENSE

Reasons for believing in a moving sun and a stationary earth

■ The sun appeared small and *looked* as if it were moving.

■ The earth felt stationary.

■ If the earth went round the sun in a year, surely a wind would sweep everything off the earth.

■ All bodies were thought to fall to the centre of the universe. Since they fall towards the centre of the earth, it seemed the earth must be central.

■ Distant stars did not seem to change position, relative to each another, as they would if the earth were moving. This effect, called parallax, was too small to be detected at the time.

Tycho Brahe, a great Danish astronomer, put forward a model of the solar system in which the sun and moon revolved around the earth at the same time as the other five known planets revolved around the sun.

Reasons for believing that the earth did not rotate

■ A cannon ball, fired straight up, would be expected to fall to the west of the firing point, because the earth would have continued spinning while the cannon ball was in the air.

■ A spinning earth would be expected to fling off everything that was not fixed to it.

■ Birds and clouds would drift steadily westwards for the same reason.

NICHOLAUS COPERNICUS

For most of his life, Copernicus was interested in astronomy. He loved to gaze up at the stars on a clear night, even though telescopes were not invented for nearly a century and a half after his birth in 1473.

Copernicus was Polish and, after his father's death, he was brought up by an uncle and later became a canon in a cathedral. He learned Greek because he wanted to know whether any of the ancient Greek astronomers had other views than the widely-accepted one of Ptolemy. Ptolemy believed that the earth was at the centre of the universe, and that the other celestial bodies circled around it.

But Copernicus found Greek astronomers who did not agree. Some of them believed in a rotating earth travelling through space. Of particular interest was a theory—a sun-centred, or heliocentric one—put forward by Aristarchos in the 3rd century BC. But the powerful influence of Aristotle's ideas was against it. Aristarchos was accused of sacrilege for displacing the earth from the centre and appearing to challenge the earth as a Divine Being.

Copernicus, too, believed the sun was at the centre. But he was reluctant to publish, not through fear of religious persecution (as is sometimes thought), but because he did not want to be laughed at.

"The scorn which I had to fear on account of the novelty and absurdity of my opinion almost drove me to abandon a work already undertaken."

Nicholaus Copernicus

As the boxed feature on the previous page shows, in those days there were better reasons for believing in a moving sun and a stationary earth than vice versa.

KEY POINTS ABOUT COPERNICUS'S THEORY

■ Copernicus's theory was attractive in that it suggested a comprehensive system, instead of Ptolemy's rather untidy scheme which treated each planet separately.

■ Contrary to one popular view, Copernicus's system did not simplify the complicated system of circles upon circles. It made it worse.

Copernicus makes matters sound simple when he says the sun is in the centre, but in his calculations the planets rotate about the *centre of the earth's orbit,* which does not coincide with the sun. Copernicus was still committed to circular motion. The idea of ellipses came with Kepler's work at the beginning of the seventeenth century. So it required a lot of circles to approximate to elliptical orbits.

■ Copernicus's book, which was to have such far-reaching effects, created little impact at the time. It was difficult to read and could only be understood by astronomers.

In 1543, *De Revolutionibus Orbium Coelestium* (On the Revolution of the Heavenly Spheres) was published. Among those friends who encouraged Copernicus to go to press were a bishop and a cardinal.

The job of seeing the book though the press was undertaken by a Lutheran minister, Andreas Osiander, known for his abilities in astronomy. Osiander advised Copernicus only to claim his theory as a *mathematical* hypothesis—a convenient calculating device—and not as a *physical* one—saying that the heavens really were like that.

The views of Aristotle and Ptolemy were so strongly entrenched that there was likely to be opposition to Copernicus's views, as well as ridicule at the seeming stupidity of a suggestion which so outraged commonsense.

Copernicus did not take Osiander's advice. He wrote as if he was convinced his world-picture was true as well as useful. And, to smooth the way, he dedicated his book to Pope Paul III.

But when the book came off the press, it was found to have an additional, anonymous preface, in front of Copernicus's own, saying,

"These views are not put forward to convince anyone that they are true, but merely to provide a correct basis for calculation."

Osiander wrote the additional words. He took an *instrumentalist* view of science (never mind whether it is true; does it work?), while Copernicus adopted a *realist* view, which sees science as finding out about something which is actually there. The difference between claiming a *mathematical hypothesis* and claiming a *physical hypothesis* was an important factor in the difficulties which arose later for Galileo.

■ Copernicus was not forced to his conclusions from scientific measurements alone. The observations he made were not particularly accurate. Copernicus's reasons for suggesting his theory were partly mystical:

"In the midst of all resides the sun. For who could place this great light in any better position . . . than that from whence it may illumine all at once?"

■ The displacement of humans from the central position was not seen by Copernicus as a threat to their uniqueness and importance to God.

"The great astronomer saw no conflict between his Christian faith and scientific activity. During his forty years as a canon, Copernicus faithfully served his church with extraordinary commitment and courage. At the same time he studied the world 'which has been built for us by the Best and Most Orderly Workman of all.'"

Dr Charles Hummel

FAREWELL TO PTOLEMY

In 1609 news reached Galileo from Holland about the invention of the telescope and he made one himself. One night he looked through it and saw what appeared to be some bright 'stars' around Jupiter. On subsequent nights he saw three, two or four 'stars'. From many nights of watching, Galileo concluded the 'stars' revolved round Jupiter.

Galileo published his findings in a book, *The Starry Messenger.* He also reported that the moon had blemishes and the Milky Way was comprised of myriads of stars. Galileo may not have been the first to have seen some of the things he describes, but he was the first to publish them. His book was short, easy to read and caused great interest. The ideas spread so rapidly that only five years later Galileo's ideas were published in Chinese by a Jesuit missionary.

Galileo used his growing fame to gain a post at the court of Cosimo II De Medici, the Fourth Grand Duke of Tuscany. Galileo wrote to tell him that he had named the four 'stars' of Jupiter the 'Medicean Stars', after him. He even went so far as to claim that God had told him to do so. He got the job he wanted and was made Chief Mathematician and Philosopher.

Hardly had *The Starry Messenger* been published when Galileo discovered Venus had phases like our moon. If Copernicus was right, and Venus went round the sun, this should happen. But if Ptolemy was right, it should not. Galileo's observations showed Ptolemy's scheme was wrong, but did not prove that Copernicus's was right. For Venus's phases also fitted in with a theory by a Danish astronomer, Tycho Brahe. His theory had a central earth, with the sun and

moon circling it, but it differed from Ptolemy's scheme in that all the other planets simultaneously circled the sun.

Galileo made a very successful visit to Rome where he was given a friendly reception by Pope Paul V. The astronomers of the Jesuit Roman College, at first unconvinced by Galileo, eventually told the head of the College, Cardinal Bellarmine, that the phases of Venus did disprove Ptolemy's theory. Galileo was publicly honoured and returned triumphant.

The Aristotelians in the universities opposed Galileo's ideas because their professional reputations were threatened. Galileo entered into some bitter arguments, including a dispute with a well-known Jesuit astronomer about who had first discovered sunspots. (Actually, neither of them was the first to publish.) Later, Galileo launched sarcastic attacks on two other Jesuits who disagreed with him. A quarter of a century later, one of them was to be the Inquisition's Commissary General at Galileo's trial.

Throughout his life Galileo used his skill in speaking and writing to pour scorn on those who disagreed with him. Even when his arguments were wrong, his tactics were very effective in making his opponents look small.

"The scientist's vanity, quarrels over priority of discovery, contemptuous attitude and effective sarcasm cost him dearly in the long run."

Dr Charles Hummel

KEY POINTS IN THE 'GALILEO AFFAIR'

■ In Galileo's day, the ideas of Aristotle and Ptolemy on physics and astronomy were accepted by professional philosophers. Disagreement could be taken as a threat to these philosophers' professional standing.

■ Greek astronomy was beginning to crumble, even before the telescope was invented. The Greeks taught that the heavens were perfect and unchanging. But the sun, viewed through a dark filter, could be seen to have spots on it, and these appeared and disappeared. In 1572 a Danish astronomer, Tycho Brahe, had seen a new star and later a comet, which seemed to cut through the 'crystalline spheres' holding the planets.

GALILEO AND THE BIBLE

Galileo's ideas posed a threat to the professional philosophers. In Rome, some of the Aristotelians united themselves to oppose Galileo. It was from their leader, Colombe, a layman, that the first opposition on religious grounds came. He claimed that various Bible texts taught the earth was central.

In 1615, Galileo wrote a long letter *'Concerning the Use of Biblical Quotations in Matters of Science'*. The letter was meant to answer theological objections to Copernicus's theory. It was also written to caution the church against making a particular view of astronomy a matter of orthodox faith, since it might later be shown to be wrong. Some extracts are given below:

" . . . in expounding the Bible if one were always to confine oneself to the unadorned grammatical meaning, one might fall into error. Not only contradictions and propositions far from true might thus be made to appear in the Bible, but even grave heresies and follies. Thus it would be necessary to assign to God feet, hands and eyes . . ."

" . . . since the Holy Ghost did not intend to teach us whether heaven moves or stands still . . . nor whether the earth is located at its centre or off to one side, then so much the less was it intended to settle for us any other conclusion of the same kind . . . Now if the Holy Spirit has purposely neglected to teach us propositions of this sort as irrelevant to the highest goal (that is, to our salvation), how can anyone affirm that it is obligatory to take sides on them? . . . I would say here something that was heard from an ecclesiastic of the most eminent degree: 'That the intention of the Holy Ghost is to teach us how one goes to heaven, not how heaven goes.' "

" . . . it being true that two truths cannot contradict one another, it is the function of wise expositors to seek out the true senses of scriptural texts. These will unquestionably accord with the physical conclusions which manifest sense and necessary demonstrations have previously made certain to us."

"I should think it would be the part of prudence not to let anyone usurp scriptural texts and force them in some way to maintain any physical conclusion to be true, when at some future time the senses . . . may show the contrary."

The letter had the opposite effect to what was intended. It stirred up trouble. Some church officials thought it was presumptuous for Galileo, a layman, to say how the Bible should be interpreted. The Catholic Church was still troubled by the effects of the Reformation, a religious movement across Europe which had challenged the authority of the Pope by appealing directly to the words of the Bible.

The general line taken by officials of the Catholic Church was to try to avoid making any official pronouncement on the Copernican theory until actual evidence was available to prove it. Galileo was reminded of the need of conclusive evidence. He promised to produce this, but never did.

Pope Paul V ordered an enquiry into how Copernicus's ideas compared with the Church's understanding of the Bible. The preliminary enquiry reported that:

"The sun is the centre of the world and completely immovable by local motion was declared unanimously to be foolish and absurd, philosophically and formally heretical inasmuch as it expressly contradicts the doctrine of Holy Scripture in many passages, both in their literal meaning and according to the general interpretation of the Fathers and Doctors."

Copernicus' book was temporarily suspended, pending a few minor changes, particularly to his preface.

The Pope told Cardinal Bellarmine to persuade Galileo to abandon his views under threat of imprisonment. What actually happened when they met is a mystery. Rumours began to circulate and Galileo asked Cardinal Bellarmine for a written report of the meeting to use in his own defence. The report said Galileo had not been forced to renounce his ideas on oath, or do penance. He had been told 'the doctrine of Copernicus, that the earth moves around the sun and that the sun is stationary in the centre of the universe and does not move from east to west, is contrary to Holy Scripture and therefore cannot be defended or held.'

And for about seven years Galileo trod cautiously.

The Reformers released the Bible to the people. But in the Roman Church the Bible was to be interpreted according to church authority. How did this affect scientific ideas?

GALILEO'S TRIAL

The events which eventually led to Galileo's trial reflect the personalities of Galileo and the new Pope, Urban VIII. One writer says of the latter that his 'vanity was indeed monumental'. His famous statement that he 'knew better than all the Cardinals put together' was only equalled by Galileo's that he alone had discovered everything new in the sky. However, it should be remembered that for a lot of the time the Pope was Galileo's friend and ally.

Galileo remained a loyal member of the Roman Catholic Church. On hearing news of the enthronement of the new Pope, there was just time for Galileo to dedicate his latest book, *The Assayer*, to him before it went to press. Urban VIII liked the book and Galileo travelled to Rome.

Galileo wanted to write a book called *Dialogue on the Flux and Reflux of the Tides*. He was convinced the tides provided concrete evidence for a moving earth—even though the astronomer Kepler had said they were caused by the moon's attraction.

The Pope insisted the treatment should remain hypothetical, the title changed to *Dialogue Concerning the Two Chief World Systems*, and his own 'unanswerable argument' be included. The Pope believed that, since God could do anything, he could have produced the tides how he liked and did not have to use the motion of the earth.

When the book was published, it clearly did not treat the issues hypothetically. And there was a sting in the tail—a most unfortunate sting. Whether it was intentional is open to question, but the Pope's views were relegated to the end of the book and put into the mouth of a character named Simplicio. 'Simplicio' is a slight, but significant change in the name of an earlier commentator on Aristotle, called Simplicius. It translates as 'simpleton'!

The Pope, who had earlier written a poem in honour of Galileo, acted swiftly. A special commission was appointed and Galileo was summoned to Rome. In the Pope's words, Galileo 'did not fear to make game of me'.

During the period of his interrogation, Galileo lived in very comfortable apartments, rather than being confined to dungeons. He was questioned about his earlier meeting with Cardinal Bellarmine and a minute of that meeting was produced from the Vatican files—a minute unknown to Galileo and shrouded in mystery. The minute was unsigned, which was irregular, but it was more strongly worded than the record from Bellarmine, who was now dead. Recent examinations of the handwriting and the watermark of the paper show the minute to correspond with other documents in the file, so it does not seem to be a later forgery and the mystery remains.

Under questioning, Galileo claimed he had not tried to defend Copernicus's views.

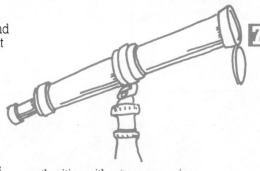

"I have neither maintained nor defended in that book the opinion that the earth moves and the sun is stationary, but have rather demonstrated the opposite of the Copernican opinion, and shown that the arguments of Copernicus are weak and not conclusive".

This was outrageously untrue and could be seen to be so by anyone who read the book, as had Galileo's inquisitors. The situation was ludicrous. Galileo's claim would never stand up in court.

Efforts were made to get an out-of-court settlement in order that it would 'be possible to deal leniently with the culprit'. Galileo claimed to have forgotten what he had written. He also offered to add to the book to disprove the Copernican system more completely. It seemed that the remainder of the trial would be a mere formality.

Then came the bombshell. Almost certainly by order of the offended Pope came the command that Galileo was to be interrogated under threat of torture. Did he, or did he not, hold the Copernican theory? But, Galileo and his inquisitors knew, it was not a threat which could be carried out, as it was illegal to torture a man aged seventy years.

Nevertheless, it was an alarming turn of events. Four times, under oath, Galileo denied holding Copernican views. The intention was to humiliate him and to make him realize that he could not ride rough-shod over the authorities without repercussions. Despite his anger, the Pope said that they would 'consult together so that he may suffer as little distress as possible'.

There the trial stopped. Galileo was sentenced to read a recantation of his Copernican views, saying that 'with sincere heart and unfeigned faith I abjure, curse, and detest the aforesaid errors and heresies'.

He was further ordered to be placed under house arrest and his prison was at first a rather sumptuous apartment at the Grand Duke's villa, then his own farm, and finally his own house in Florence. By permission, even the penance of daily reciting Psalms was delegated to a nun, one of three children Galileo had had by his mistress.

LESSONS FROM GALILEO

Many attempts have been made to decide what were the key issues which led to the 'Galileo Affair'. Folklore often presents it as 'science versus religion'. But this is not the case.

"Although Galileo was not deeply spiritual, he was sincerely religious and a loyal churchman. The celebrated Galileo case, therefore, does not truly revolve about the perennial issues of science versus religion."
Dr Raymond Seeger

At various times, Galileo received much support and encouragement from church leaders. However, a key factor was the very sensitive issue of who could interpret the Bible in the wake of the 'Counter Reformation', as the Roman Catholic Church's response to the Reformation is often called. The decree at the Council of Trent was that the ultimate authority for the interpretation of the Bible belongs to the Church Fathers.

Galileo was presuming to interpret it himself in the light of the world around.

So Galileo had argued for an (approximately) heliocentric universe, the Catholic Church for a geocentric one. But how does the controversy look from our present understanding of spacetime?

"Galileo said that the earth moves and the sun is fixed; the Inquisition said that that the earth is fixed and the sun moves; and Newtonian astronomers, adopting an absolute theory of space, said that both the sun and the earth move. But now we say that any one of these three statements is equally true, provided that you have fixed your sense of 'rest' and 'motion'."
Professor A.N.Whitehead

But scientific ideas are constantly changing. Future generations may view things quite differently.

PART EIGHT: EVOLUTION AND CREATION

The study of human origins has often caused a storm. Theories quickly get extended to embrace morality, politics and religion.

■ **If we developed from other animals, is there anything special about us?**

■ **If we evolved over aeons of time, can we really be 'made in the image of God'?**

■ **If 'survival of the fittest' was the route by which we progressed from protozoa to people, was Hitler wrong to think he could advance evolution by weeding out the weak through death camps?**

■ **If the earth is really four billion years old, what do the 'six days' of creation mean?**

Theories of evolution have been around for centuries. But we focus on Charles Darwin in the last century because he was the first to come up with a plausible way by which evolution could have occurred. Before Darwin it was very speculative. After Darwin it looked more like fact.

A distinction needs to be made between **evolution**—the fact that changes take place from generation to generation, which is generally accepted by biologists; and the **mechanisms** by which changes occur —a matter of continuing debate. Darwin's theory is about the

mechanisms of change. It is based on certain assumptions.

■ **Living things reproduce freely in the wild, resulting in competition for the available food and space.**

■ **Animals prey on each other.**

■ **Offspring are not exactly like their parents.**

■ **Many characteristics are inherited, though Darwin had no idea how (the idea of genes came later).**

■ **The longest-living members of species are likely to reproduce the most.**

Darwin's theory holds that some variations, like longer legs or different-shaped beaks, may give a better chance of survival against predators or food shortage. And if the last two of the above assumptions are true, more of the population will come to possess such characteristics.

OPPORTUNITY OF A LIFETIME!

Charles Darwin was born in England in 1809, the son of a doctor. As a student he started to study medicine, but was put off by watching operations performed without anaesthetics. He went to Cambridge University to prepare to be a minister in the Church of England. But his real interest was natural history and, through his friendship with Professor Henslow, a botanist, Darwin became ship's naturalist to *HMS Beagle*. Setting sail in 1831, HMS *Beagle* was to begin a five-year voyage round the world.

Darwin held the widely accepted

Charles Darwin developed an interest in the natural world as a student, although his course was originally in medicine.

belief that God had separately created different species with characteristics suited to their environments. A giraffe had a long neck to reach its food, and a polar bear had a thick coat to keep warm. Within any one species the differences between individuals were usually small, and hybrids were generally sterile. It seemed unlikely that one species could ever change into another.

A second, religious reason, to doubt that one species could evolve into another, arose from one reading of Genesis. Although it did not specifically say there were no links between the different 'kinds' of God's creation, neither did it say there were. Many people thought this meant each species was separately created.

Later Darwin said that during the voyage 'vague doubts occasionally flitted across my mind', whether species were fixed. The year after he returned he wrote,

"I am almost convinced (quite contrary to the opinion I started with) that species are not (it is like confessing to a murder) immutable."

Many people believed the world had been created in 4004BC. But Charles Lyell, later Darwin's friend, and a number of other eminent geologists thought the earth was a lot older than six thousand years. If that were so, then over much longer periods of time, lots of little changes within a species *might* add up to big ones. One species might gradually evolve into another.

Darwin wrote out a short version of

HMS Beagle, the ship on which Darwin was ship's naturalist, made a journey to South America to chart the coastline.

his 'species theory' in 1842. Lyell tried to persuade Darwin to publish, in case he should be beaten to it, but Darwin wanted more time.

In June 1858 Darwin received a letter from a fellow naturalist, Alfred Wallace, working in Malaya. Wallace had hit upon the same ideas as Darwin and wanted help in getting them published. Darwin wrote to Lyell,

"I never saw a more striking coincidence: if Wallace had my manuscript sketch written out in 1842 he could not have made a better short abstract!"

Lyell quickly arranged for Wallace's paper and one by Darwin to be read jointly to the Linnean Society on 1st July. It attracted little interest. The President, in his report for that year, said 'The year—has not been marked by any of those striking discoveries which revolutionize the department of science on which they bear'!

The pressure was on Darwin to publish in more detail. Instead of the mammoth work he planned, he published a sizeable volume, *The Origin of Species*, the following year.

Darwin challenged the fixity of species and although he hardly mentioned humans in the *Origin*, the implications were obvious. These were developed in his later book, *The Descent of Man*. His ideas got a mixed reception from fellow scientists and from the public at large.

HOW DID DARWIN GET HIS THEORY?

Evolutionary ideas go back long before Darwin. His important contributions were to suggest a plausible mechanism and to produce a wealth of evidence in support. By analogy with 'artificial selection' he called the mechanism 'natural selection'.

The term 'natural selection' can be misleading because

■ **the process is not a 'selection' of certain characteristics but an 'elimination' of others;**

■ **'nature' is not a person, who 'selects'.**

One difficulty that Darwin's theory could not cope with was why characteristics, which could be enhanced by breeding, did not die out in the wild by becoming 'diluted'. Darwin had a theory of *blending inheritance* by which mating between pairs, one of which had a particular characteristic and the other not, resulted in each offspring having a reduced amount. It could be compared to mixing clean water with

MALTHUS

Darwin's thinking was influenced by *artificial selection*, used for breeding racehorses and dogs. To get a different-looking dog or a faster racehorse, the owners selected for breeding only those animals with the right characteristics. After many generations, they were able to establish, within limits, the changes they wanted. In captivity the process was clear, but Darwin was not sure how changes could be 'selected' for further breeding in the wild.

A significant input to Darwin's thinking came from reading a book by Thomas Malthus, an Anglican clergyman. Malthus argued that, because populations tend to increase faster than available food supplies, there will always be a struggle for existence. Darwin wrote,

"It at once struck me that under these circumstances favourable variations would tend to be preserved and unfavourable ones to be destroyed. The result of this would be the formation of a new species. Here, then, I had at last got a theory by which to work".

blue ink. The resulting liquid is pale blue.

The development of genetics in the twentieth century changed this view. Applied to Darwin's ideas it led to the New Synthesis, or Neo-Darwinism. On this theory, mating could be compared to mixing two heaps of variously coloured counters—representing the genes. The collection is separated out into new heaps—the offspring, which either contain particular coloured counters or not.

Where the genetic information results in creatures which are better fitted to survive and reproduce, the genes are carried into future generations.

8 THE IMPACT OF THE 'ORIGIN'

Folklore has it that Darwin's theory was welcomed by the scientists and opposed by the religious. The history of science shows this popular belief to be wrong. The scientists were in many cases religious people themselves, so attempts to line up 'the scientists' on one side and 'the religious' on the other present difficulties.

"The truth is nearer to the exact opposite: it was a few theologians and many scientists who dismissed Darwinism and evolution."
Dr James Moore

At that time there were many good scientific reasons for not accepting Darwin's theory. Darwin himself was aware of these objections, listed them and tried to find answers. Samuel Wilberforce, Bishop of Oxford, stated many of them in a review of the

Origin, which Darwin referred to as 'uncommonly clever; it picks out with skill all the most conjectural parts, and brings forward well all the difficulties'. The Bishop's review was devoted almost entirely to scientific criticisms and his summing up paints a very different picture to the popular view of an obscurantist clergyman opposing science for religious reasons.

"We have objected to the views with which we are dealing solely on scientific grounds . . . We think that all objections (which oppose facts of nature because they contradict revelation) savour of a timidity which is really inconsistent with a firm and well-intrusted faith."
Samuel Wilberforce, Bishop of Oxford

Wilberforce repeated some of his arguments in an encounter with Thomas Huxley at a meeting which has become a legend. Huxley was a young scientist, a friend of Darwin, and a supporter of the new evolutionary ideas. The meeting of the British Association for the Advancement of Science which took place in Oxford in 1860 is surrounded by folklore. The records of what took place are scarce; and what records there are vary in their reliability.

Bishop Wilberforce was a skilful orator, well able to use his powers of speech destructively. He was not popular and seems to have made some indiscreet remark about 'apes' and 'grandmothers'. Whatever was said it does not seem to have caused any great stir.

"It is a significant fact that the famous clash between Huxley and the Bishop was not reported by a single London newspaper at the time."
Dr Alvar Ellegard

Stories of this kind make good entertainment. The very scarcity of historical detail gives abundant scope for the imagination.

In Darwin's time there were strong currents of feeling against the Church of England, for social reasons. As some of the new scientists sought a voice for themselves and their science, they used the Wilberforce-Huxley skirmish as an example of the supposed ignorance of the church. In later years the importance of the Oxford encounter was much exaggerated. It became a legend.

In fact, throughout the whole

Thomas Huxley and Bishop Wilberforce argued on opposite sides at a famous British Association meeting which debated Darwin's ideas.

DARWIN'S RELIGIOUS BELIEFS

Darwin was reticent about his own religious beliefs. Popular accounts of Darwin's life often claim the pure and simple truth was that he gradually gave them up on account of his science. Oscar Wilde once remarked that 'the truth is rarely pure and never simple'. For Darwin, it would be more accurate to say that there were mutual interactions between his religious beliefs and his scientific theory. He was already rejecting Christianity because he found the idea of hell unpalatable.

Darwin also had doubts about the Bible and rejected miracles, saying, 'the more we know of the fixed laws of nature the more incredible do miracles become'. But, according to one historian, it was the death of his child Annie that did the damage.

"Despite the fluctuation of his religious beliefs, in both content and strength, a fairly consistent position does emerge. 'In my most extreme fluctuations,' he wrote, 'I have never been an Atheist in the sense of denying the existence of a God' . . . And on the positive side, he seems to have retained an 'inward conviction' that the universe as a whole could not be the product of chance."
Dr John Brooke

evolution debate, there have always been Christians both for and against Darwin's views. When *Origin* was published, some Christians welcomed it as a further step in tracing how God had created the world.

8 CREATION AND EVOLUTION: SOME ISSUES

A distinction needs to be made between evolution—that changes take place from generation to generation—and the mechanisms by which these changes occur. Evolution is generally accepted by biologists, but the mechanisms are a matter of continued debate.

In Darwin's days there were scientific objections to his theory.

■ **Was there really time for variations to accumulate?**

■ **Could an animal go on changing or, as with artificial selection, was there a limit?**

■ **If a single animal changed, would the new improvement survive, or would it be swamped by interbreeding with animals without it?**

Over the last 150 years many of these objections have been answered. The earth is thought to be 4,600 million years old, fossils are said to point to intermediate stages, and new theories of genetics show how changes pass down through many generations. With this additional understanding, we call the theory neo-Darwinism.

It is generally agreed there are changes on a small scale, such as the appearance of new varieties. This is often called micro-evolution.

But claims of large changes over long periods, or macro-evolution, have caused some religious people to feel uneasy. They wonder whether these ideas contradict the Bible.

They are concerned to understand:

■ **The idea of creation, in view of evolution;**

■ **The six 'days' of Genesis;**

■ **The Adam and Eve accounts in Genesis;**

■ **The 'kinds' of Genesis and whether species were separately created;**

■ **The Bible's claim that people are made 'in the image of God'.**

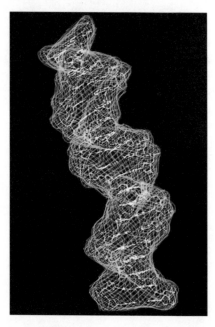

Darwin knew nothing about genes or the DNA molecule. More recent discoveries have led to refinements of his theories.

But the debate is only just begun with questions on how we understand the early chapters of Genesis. It also covers the whole idea of change and evolution. Does the theory suggest that humanity itself is moving onward and upward?

On the more negative side, is evolution wasteful and cruel? A question like this is part of the much larger issue of why there is evil in the world. The problem is sometimes put in the rather slick form of saying that God cannot be all-powerful and all-good. For if he were both then he would stop evil. If he wants to stop it, but cannot, then he is not all-powerful. If he is all-powerful, but does not stop it then he cannot be all-good. As a piece of rhetoric it trips neatly off the tongue, but fails to do justice to logical constraints.

If love is to be of prime value in the world, then there must be freedom. It is a contradiction in terms to speak of 'forcing' someone to love somebody else. Love is an act of free choice. So, if a creator wants creatures who can love, he has to give them the freewill not to love, if they so wish. That brings in the possibility of evil. To ask, 'why doesn't God make people who are bound to love him?' is to use a meaningless combination of words.

Much of the evil in the world is the result of human sin. This is more obviously the case when we think of hatred, selfishness and greed than it is when we consider earthquakes, storms and other natural disasters. But even here there may be human failing.

Two of the words which the Bible uses for 'sin' have the meanings, respectively, of 'transgression' and 'missing the mark'. The first conveys the idea of active disobedience—of crossing over a forbidden boundary. The second indicates the falling short of some standard—of failing to match up to what is required. Part of the original command to subdue the earth may have meant the control of natural forces, perhaps as Jesus did with the storm on the lake of Galilee. But so much is conjecture. We simply do not know what the world would have been like if sin had not entered it. However, in addition to the evils consequent upon human failure, it needs to be borne in mind that the Bible also speaks of spiritual powers of wickedness.

"Meaningless combinations of words do not suddenly acquire meaning simply because we prefix to them the two other words 'God can' . . . It is no more possible for God than for the weakest of his creatures to carry out both of two mutually exclusive alternatives; not because his power meets an obstacle, but because nonsense remains nonsense even when we talk it about God."

Professor C.S.Lewis

CREATION IN THE BIBLE

Before trying to decide whether or not creation is a rival to evolution, we need to look at what is meant by 'creation'.

The word 'creation' can be used of a fashion designer's *creation* of a new dress, a pop group's *creation* of a new style of music, or about the physical beginnings of our universe. It carries the idea of bringing something new into existence which was not there before.

The means that are used, or the length of time it takes, do not affect the *fact* of creation. As has been said, 'Mozart composed his music with great rapidity; Beethoven sometimes laboured for years over a single composition'. Yet the difference in the time they took does not make the music of one more worthwhile than that of the other.

In its religious sense, 'creation' takes on the additional meaning of 'bringing-into-being-by-*God*'.

The first people to use the Genesis creation story lived in a society where there were many other creation stories. The stories involved gods at war, battles between good and evil, and lesser gods being given the job of creation. The main aim of Genesis is to declare that creation is the work of one God, and that it is good.

Creation, here, is not constructing something out of pre-existing materials. It means bringing into existence everything there is— sometimes called *creatio ex nihilo*. So the story starts, 'In the beginning . . .', and not 'Once upon a time'. Time itself is part of the creation and so is space. The Big Bang was not the expansion of a fireball into already existing space, but the expansion of spacetime itself.

Having said that, the Bible places little emphasis on the formation of space and time. The idea of creation is much more about relationships. Genesis stresses that everything, ourselves included, is absolutely dependent upon God, and therefore places its emphasis on attitudes and behaviour.

A few scientists initially opposed the 'Big Bang' theory because they disliked the idea of a creating God. But 'creation' as 'bringing into being' is independent of *how* the universe came into existence. At present the Big Bang theory is preferred, but that may change.

CONTINUOUS CREATION

Before the Big Bang theory became widely accepted there was a 'steady-state theory', sometimes called the 'continuous-creation theory'. The theory said that hydrogen atoms were being continually formed in space, at a rate of one per cubic metre every 300,000 years, to make up for those that were moving away in an expanding universe. Some people, including those who put the theory forward, imagined it ruled out the idea of a creating God. But, as one professor pointed out, it did not. It simply replaced one 'big bang' with a lot of 'little pops'.

Even if, on our time scale, we concluded the universe was infinitely old, that still would not deny its being 'brought into being' by God. For creation is an act outside of time. As Augustine expressed it in the fifth century, creation is *with* time, not *in* time.

QUESTIONS ON GENESIS

There are three questions people keep asking:

Only six days?

"The poor world is almost six thousand years old."
William Shakespeare, *As You Like It*

Some people (notably Archbishop Ussher) thought you could calculate the age of the earth by adding up all the ages in the family trees in the Bible. The creation date came to 4004BC. For a while this figure was included in the margins of Bibles.

However, the family trees in the Bible are incomplete, and the discovery of fossils in rock strata when digging canals at the time of the industrial revolution suggested the earth was much older.

But long before evidence for an ancient earth was available, church leaders such as Augustine interpreted the 'days' of Genesis differently. It was not that new meanings of 'days' arose simply because of nineteenth-century discoveries in geology. The text itself provided clues. It did not need much insight to see that, with light appearing on day one and the sun on day four, the writer probably did not intend the sequence to be understood chronologically, but topically. Thus

Day 1 Light created and separated from darkness
Day 2 Sky created, separating the waters
Day 3 Sea and land separated and vegetation created
Day 4 Lights (sun, moon and stars) created to inhabit the heavens and rule over day and night
Day 5 Birds and sea creatures created to inhabit the sky and the waters
Day 6 Animals and people created to inhabit the land

Those who continue to understand the days chronologically have variously taken them to mean geological ages, days of revelation to the writer, rotations of the earth about its axis, and figurative days (as in 'Napoleon's day').

Were Adam and Eve real people?

Adam and Eve have been variously understood as,

■ referring to two actual people,

■ representatives of the human race,

■ expressions of the truth about the relationship of people to God—or all three.

Certain passages bear the interpretation simply of Adam and Eve as representatives of humanity. But there are others which appear to go further and to present them as two people. So how would this fit in with the evolutionary development of *homo sapiens*? Perhaps the story of Cain and Abel gives the smallest of clues. When God calls Cain to account for the murder of his brother Cain replies, 'I will be a homeless wanderer on the earth, and anyone who finds me will kill me.' But Cain's

father is Adam, so who are those who may kill Cain?

"The tendency to assume that the Genesis account is so simple and artless that anyone can comprehend it at first glance appears to be very widespread".
Professor Douglas Spanner

Some believe that the account of Adam and Eve starting at Genesis chapter 2 verse 4 contradicts the one given in the verses leading up to that because of the differences in sequence. This does not necessarily follow. The criticism assumes the intention *is* to give chronological accounts. It may not be. The second account of Adam and Eve can be taken like a television documentary which, after giving a panoramic view in chapter 1, zooms in on one central feature, namely human beings.

Made in the image of God?

Being made in the image of God includes our spiritual awareness, that we are capable of a relationship with God, best described as 'personal'. It is seen in ways in which we reflect qualities attributed to God, such as creativity.

One issue raised by evolution was whether the 'lowly origins' of animal ancestry cut across this grand picture of bearing God's likeness. But the 'image of God' does not refer to physical form or bodily ancestry, for 'God is Spirit', not flesh and blood. The Bible puts our origins even lower, 'for dust you are and to dust you will return'.

EVOLUTION AND/OR CREATION?

Some people use 'creation' to mean something more than 'bringing-into-being-by-God'. They use it as shorthand for 'Special Creation', the claim not only that God created, but that he did so *in a series of separate acts*. These people are often called 'creationists'.

■ **Creationists do not believe God created the world through slow evolutionary processes, but using sudden, all-powerful miracles. The world, they mostly believe, is only about 10,000 years old. They have developed geological and biological theories to support their beliefs.**

■ **The label 'creationist' is associated almost exclusively with those who hold these *extra* beliefs. Other people also believe that God created everything—and could therefore properly be called 'creationists'. But they accept evolution as the mechanism, which so-called 'creationists' deny.**

■ **Creationists claim they obtain their views directly from the Bible. Like all interpreters, they understand Genesis in a particular way. For them it is an account which records the events (and their order) of a single creation week. Others, equally committed to believing in a God of creation, understand the intention of Genesis in a different, and less literal, way.**

■ **Many people who are unsympathetic to religion imagine that showing the inadequacies of 'creationist' biology and geology disproves creation rather than**

creation*ism*. **The 'ism' part needs to be carefully distinguished.**

"Much of the energy of the creationist movement arises from a sense of moral outrage at the advance of an evolution-centred world-view that has the audacity to parade its secular, liberal values as if they were the objective findings of science. Here at least, if not in matters of biological fact and theory, creationism has a point of which the scientific community might do well to take heed."
Professor John Durant

Creation is an *act*—the act of an agent, in this case God. Evolution is a *process.*
  A description of the *processes* of creation is not a logical alternative to the *act* of creation, as Darwin himself realized. But, he said, it is very easily done, for 'the habit of looking for one kind of meaning I suppose deadens the perception of another'.
  Nobody would claim that understanding the mechanisms of an invention ruled out an inventor. Yet a similar claim is made that understanding the mechanisms of creation rules out a Creator.

"The most persistent misapprehension about God and creation, however, is that knowledge of causal mechanism automatically excludes any possibility that God is acting in a particular situation."
Professor Sam Berry

Careless expressions like 'evolution *did* it' treat evolution as though it were a *cause*—or even a person—which it is not. Sometimes there is the veiled implication, '..therefore not God'. It is used to claim there is no plan or purpose behind creation.

Although evolution does not show there *is* a creating God, it certainly does not show there is *not*.

THE MISUSE OF EVOLUTIONARY THEORY

Darwin claimed that evolution worked through a struggle for survival. In any animal or plant environment there is always competition: competition for food, for light, for space. In the struggle, only the 'fittest' will survive.

Victorian society prospered on industrial competition. Workers were paid low wages while their bosses became rich. People also speculated on (or assumed) which nation was 'the fittest', and how the human race could be advanced by selective breeding. Evolution in nature was seen as a key to unlock future human prosperity and success.

Because Adolf Hitler appealed to the 'survival of the fittest' for his 'master race', evolution has been called evil. This is a bad argument. Misuse does not necessarily make something bad in itself. Nobel's invention of dynamite was a splendid way of making an unstable explosive, nitroglycerine, safe for quarrying. But Nobel was so horrified at the misuses of dynamite that he gave some of his fortune to establish the Nobel Peace Prize.

'RED IN TOOTH AND CLAW'?

The ideologies which based themselves on competition in nature have overplayed the idea of struggle, and have neglected aspects of evolution which contradict their beliefs.

"'The survival of the fittest' no longer implies a gladiatorial view of nature, for survival now means reproductive success; not the conqueror, but the parent with the largest number of progeny reaching parenthood, is the fittest."
Professor Ian Barbour

In a poem published a few years before Origin of Species, Alfred Lord Tennyson used the phrase 'Nature, red in tooth and claw'. His words are really an overstatement, made at a time when biology was not so well understood. Some conflict in nature ends in submission, not death. There is symbiosis, in which organisms depend on each other, as well as competition. There is also altruism, where individuals give up their lives for other members of their species.

ONWARD AND UPWAR

Evolution has been said to imply human moral progress, which seems to contradict Bible teaching about the human race falling into sin and needing forgiveness.

Darwin, normally very careful in his writings, made an extravagant claim on almost the last page of the Origin:

"Hence we may look with some confidence to a secure future of great length. And as natural selection works solely by and for the good of each being, all corporeal and mental endowments will tend to progress towards perfection."

'Progress' is not a word which can stand on its own. Progress is always towards some desired goal. In the world of nature, that goal is simply survival through being better adapted to the

The Victorian Capitalists tried to justify cut-throat competition in business from evolution, while Communism seized upon the idea of biological struggle to try to justify violent revolution. The way Victorian Capitalism, Nazism and Communism have each claimed to follow from evolution should arouse suspicion, for it is difficult to imagine three more incompatible ideologies. With such diverse conclusions, they cannot all logically follow from the same scientific theory.

These ideologies could only claim scientific backing if biology could show us what we *ought* to do. It can't.

It can only describe what is already there. Attempts to arrive at 'evolutionary ethics' fall into the is/ought fallacy. There is no valid way of getting to what *ought* to be done from what the world *is* like. Some moral dimension has to be added as well. It does not follow that, because there is competition and struggle in nature, people are justified in doing each other down in gas chambers, cut-throat business or violent revolutions.

environment than other organisms. No other characteristics, of a moral or religious nature, which are counted worthwhile by any other criteria than survival and reproduction, are involved.

"The types which survive are deemed to be valuable by no criterion other than the fact of their survival."
Professor C.E.M. Joad

The idea of evolutionary progress provided a common meeting ground for the Jesuit, Pierre Teilhard de Chardin, and the humanist biologist, Sir Julian Huxley. Despite very different ideas about God, Huxley wrote an enthusiastic preface to Teilhard's The Phenomenon of Man. In an obituary of Huxley, it was said that he 'made a religion of evolution'.

"In the past, attempts to derive optimistic lessons from biology concerning the future of humankind have owed far more to prior religious or political convictions than they have to any independent insights derived from science; and, as the example of Julian Huxley illustrates, this has been the case even where those involved have been major authorities on Darwinism. There is nothing in a scientific training, it would seem, that immunizes a person against their own prejudices."
Professor John Durant

BIOLOGY AND BEHAVIOUR

Courses of action are sometimes claimed to be right because they are 'natural'. But although the word natural is often used approvingly, it does not follow that what is natural is necessarily right. What is called 'natural' by us imperfect human beings is not necessarily what was 'natural' in the world as God intended it. It may be 'natural' to hit someone if they hit you, but that does not make it right. It is natural for humans to want to mate, but that does not make it right for a man to take any woman he fancies.

Human behaviour is affected by heredity and environment: by 'nature' through our genes and by 'nurture' through our upbringing. But we are not bound by natural selection, and we may go against it. The weak and the aged are not exterminated by struggle, but are often cared for. The human race freely chooses to control

Professor Julian Huxley was a leading exponent of 'evolutionary humanism', the view that humanity will evolve to the 'better' life.

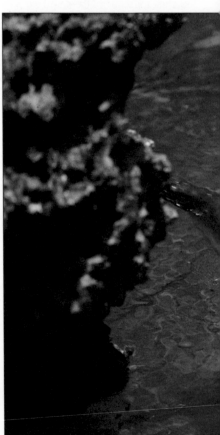

its development and environment, rather than being helplessly carried along by it.

Not everyone agrees with this point about freedom of choice. Some take a much stronger line than simply saying we are 'affected' or 'influenced' by nature or nurture. They claim we are completely *determined* by them.

Sociobiology claims all behaviour is determined by genes and reproductive advantage. Sociology, in an extreme form, claims we are totally determined by our environment. In sociobiology religious beliefs are interpreted as having survival value by making the believers biologically fitter. In sociology the beliefs are judged on their social function. In neither case is the truth or falsity of the beliefs counted relevant.

But both theories trip themselves up if they deny the relevance of truth. For if beliefs (and these theories are beliefs) are only held because they have survival value or are the result of social conditioning, why should anyone accept them? Neither theory does justice to the role of human reason.

Are there differences between the development of the human species and other species? Do humans have more influence on their destiny?

PART NINE: ACCIDENT OR DESIGN?

Almost everybody stops occasionally to admire the beauty of the natural world: the colours of a sunset, the delicacy of a flower, the marvel of a new-born baby.

But are we deceiving ourselves when we turn from creation to Creator, and say that God designed the world? If the intricate and beautiful aspects of nature arose by natural selection, can we still say God planned it?

THE ARGUMENT FROM DESIGN

While at Cambridge, Darwin was impressed by the writings of the mathematician and theologian William Paley. Paley said if he found a stone on a heath he would attach no significance to it. But if he found a watch he would conclude it was something made for a purpose.

Paley then argued from a human invention pointing to a designer, to the world pointing to a Designer. The argument from design was based on the way every creature seemed fitted for its environment. The way all the parts of a watch fit together is evidence of a skilled watchmaker; the intricacies of nature are evidence of God. This approach suffers from the defects of any argument from analogy, but it has persuasive force.

Darwin maintained there had not been separate creations, but evolution from various forms. He saw this as more fitting for God's activity, and his famous summing up of *Origin of Species* makes the point:

"There is grandeur in this view of life, with its separate powers, having been originally breathed by the Creator into a few forms or into one; and that, while this planet has gone cycling on according to the fixed law of gravity, from so simple a beginning endless forms most beautiful and most wonderful have been and are being evolved."

However, the 'design' now appeared to be natural selection 'weeding out' living things less fitted for survival and reproduction. This seemed a wasteful and haphazard procedure,

unlikely to be used by human designers, let alone God. So it was not so much *evolution*, but Darwin's mechanism of *natural selection* that was distasteful.

Interestingly, such a mechanism of chance variations followed by a selection procedure, called 'Darwinian Design', is now used to produce such things as efficient aerofoil sections for wind generators.

Darwin is sometimes said to have destroyed the argument from design. This is only partially true. Certainly, evolution by natural selection did cut across the idea of a multitude of separate creations. But since the biblical accounts did not necessarily

The intricacy of nature seems to suggest a designer.

imply separate creations, this is not a particular difficulty.

It could still be argued that since complex living creatures exist (by whatever processes), so design is still a possibility. Darwin's own comparison of natural selection and human selection could imply that intelligence works through nature, much as intelligence worked through pigeon enthusiasts breeding pigeons. Darwin conceded in a letter:

"I can see no reason why a man, or other animal, may not have been expressly designed by an omniscient (all-seeing) Creator, who foresaw every future event and consequence."

In one way it is odd that evolution should have caused religious objections. For it can be seen as re-emphasizing something lost sight of in deism: God does not occasionally 'interfere', but is continually active. For any theory of God's occasional intervention would also imply his 'ordinary absence'.

Charles Kingsley, author of *The Water Babies*, was enthusiastic over Darwin's theory for this reason. He said, 'they find that now they have got

Archdeacon Paley argued that if we find a watch on a heath we are sure to suppose it was made for a purpose.

rid of an interfering God—a master-magician, as I call it—they have to choose between the absolute empire of accident, and a living, immanent, ever-working God.'

But, apart from these modifications to earlier forms of the design argument, there were other ways in which design could be claimed. One, expressed by Malthus and favoured by Darwin, was that the laws of nature themselves were designed. After all, it could be claimed that laws pointed to a Lawgiver no less than design pointed to a Designer. So, because of the design of these laws, living things *had* to arise.

The matter of design has recently attracted fresh attention over the so-called Anthropic Principle. The physical constraints of nature are so 'finely tuned' that, were they slightly different, we should not be here. This is entirely consistent with God planning the universe with people in mind. It is, however, unwise to try to make a knock-down argument for God from it, as other interpretations are possible.

A CHANCY BUSINESS

We often say things happen 'by chance'. But what do we mean?

■ **"I bumped into John by chance this morning,"** said Karen when she returned from the shops.

■ **"The universe can emerge out of nothing, without intervention, by chance,"** writes Dr Peter Atkins.

In both cases the word 'chance' is used to deny plan or purpose. Using this meaning, Darwin spoke of the 'impossibility of conceiving that this grand wondrous universe, with our conscious selves, arose through chance'.

A difficulty of being sure there *is* no plan behind 'chance' events arises from our limited knowledge. Karen would have been wrong in thinking her encounter with John was unplanned if John liked her, knew she went shopping every Saturday morning and walked round town till he 'bumped into her'.

■ **"At the deepest level, purpose vanishes and is replaced by the consequences of having the opportunity to explore at random,"** writes Dr Atkins.

He uses 'random', as he used 'chance', to deny any God-given purpose to the universe. But the same difficulty of not knowing everything still applies.

CHANCE OR NOT?

Look at these three sets of letters:

1. fcuidvlgvpdgjfrjllcolysmdapcbuud

Produced by selecting repeated single letters on a keyboard while blindfold. Completely unplanned. Any letter had a 1 in 26 chance of coming up at any selection.

2. jkdleuhitehaoarcedndohcwnicemiae

Constructed from every third letter of a common nursery rhyme. Whatever the appearance, only one letter, in each position, fits the planned sequence.

3. uijtajtabatfoufodfajoafbtzadpef

Each letter in a simple sentence is replaced by the following letter in the alphabet to give a simple code. At the ends, z becomes a space and a space becomes a. Again, each letter is necessary in that position. (A cryptologist might have become interested by the frequency of f's and a's and started looking for a solution.)

No one believing the sequences were unplanned would have wasted time looking for any significance. That is only worthwhile if there is a rational mind behind it and it is intelligible.

The difficulty about not being 'in the know' surrounds all our judgments of randomness. We may deny the *appearance* of a plan in chance processes or random events. But we are not in a position to deny the *existence* of a plan unless we have all the facts, as a final example will show: A convenient way of obtaining a random set of digits is to go down a page of a telephone directory, taking the last digit from each entry. Anyone ignorant of the source of the random digits might think they were unplanned.

9 A COSMIC ACCIDENT?

Suppose the universe *was* unplanned. If we, and that includes our brains, are just accidents, are there any guarantees that the thoughts we think can be relied on? We have to assume they can, or we cannot even discuss the matter. But we could be living under a delusion, with no means of knowing it:

"If my mental processes are determined wholly by the motions of the atoms in my brain, I have no reason to suppose that my beliefs are true . . . and hence I have no reason for supposing my brain to be composed of atoms."
Professor J.B.S.Haldane

Some years ago, Jacques Monod, molecular biologist and Nobel prizewinner, wrote a popular book, *Chance and Necessity*. In it he expressed personal beliefs about the universe alongside the biology. He concluded with the dramatic claim:

"Man at last knows that he is alone in the unfeeling immensity of the universe, out of which he emerged only by chance. Neither his destiny nor his duty have been written down."

Monod's personal beliefs caused interest in a way they might not have done, had he not been an eminent biologist. But, as has often been pointed out since, his beliefs do not follow from his biology. It is sometimes stated that:

"The biological meaning of chance is that mutations happen regardless of whether they will be useful to the species when they occur, or ever."
Professor Theodore Dobzhansky

This is a working assumption, made by biologists, but nothing more. As Professor Douglas Spanner, another biologist, asks, 'What evidence can they produce in support of this claim, *quite fundamental to their whole position?* Can they even outline an operational procedure which might, in principle, establish it?'

One difficulty about Monod's belief that everything is the result of chance is that the belief itself would be the result of chance. So also would be the belief of those who think the opposite!

As distinct from popular usage, 'chance' and 'random' are used precisely in science. The confusion arising when a popular meaning ('unplanned') is given to the word 'chance' in its technical sense is matched by the confusion arising when a technical meaning ('species') is given to a word ('kinds') used in a popular sense.

How should we understand the changes that happen in living cells? If they are random, does this mean there can be no purpose?

WHAT IS CHANCE?

'Chance' and 'random' are used in a scientific sense about events whose outcomes cannot be predicted, such as

1. throwing dice;
2. tossing coins;
3. radioactive decay.

We say it is a matter of *chance* as to which side comes uppermost in (**1**) and (**2**), and that the sequence of heads and tails in (**2**) is *random*. In (**3**) the breakdown of atoms occurs *at random* and it is a matter of *chance* as to which one breaks down next.

Although individual random events like radioactive decays are unpredictable, the behaviour of large numbers of such events is highly predictable and law-like. Large numbers of randomly-colliding gas molecules fit in with a regular pattern of behaviour, described by Boyle's Law.

'Laws of chance' are as important in science as other laws. As a President of the Royal Society remarked, 'there are few laws more precise than those of perfect molecular chaos'. Like other laws in science, the 'laws of chance' do not dictate events, they only describe them. They say what to expect in a long sequence, *not* in an individual case.

The fact that events such as mutations or radioactive decays are presently unpredictable does not mean they have no physical cause, though this is sometimes claimed for certain events in quantum mechanics. The difficulty with such a claim is that there is no way of distinguishing between events which have no cause and events whose causes are presently unknown. Even if it turned out that some events had no physical cause, this would not necessarily deny divine activity. It could mean that God had not acted on the usual (physical) cause and effect basis.

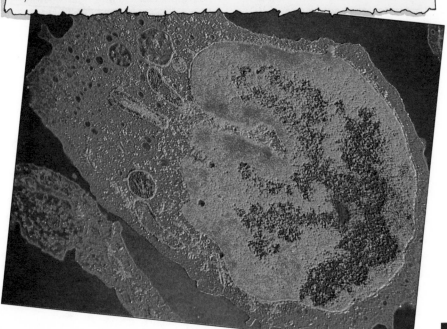

LADY LUCK

'Chance' is sometimes used in popular speech as though it were the *cause* of something happening:

"Chance is operating by causing these random changes, mutations, in the underlying genetic recipe."

Dr Richard Dawkins

Sometimes 'chance' is even spoken about as though it were a person— 'Lady Luck'—able to think, plan and create, instead of simply a concept. This way of speaking, called 'Tychism' after the Greek goddess of chance, is seen in another of Dr Dawkins' claims:

"Chance *with* natural selection, chance smeared out into innumerable tiny steps over aeons of time, *is* powerful enough to manufacture miracles like dinosaurs and ourselves."

It can be misleading to talk about chance like this, even if it is only claimed to be a figure of speech. 'Chance' gets personified and 'begins to play God'. The oddity of treating 'chance' (absence of an identifiable cause) as though it were a person has been compared to treating 'nobody' (absence of a person) as though it were a person, as happens in Lewis Carroll's *Alice Through the Looking Glass*:

" 'I see nobody on the road,' said Alice. 'I only wish *I* had such eyes,' the King remarked in a fretful tone. 'To be able to see Nobody! And at that distance too.' . . . 'Who did you pass on the road?' the King went on, holding out his hand to the Messenger for some more hay. 'Nobody,' said the Messenger. 'Quite right,' said the King, 'this young lady saw him too.' "

Other concepts, as well as 'chance', get treated as though they were secular substitutes for God: 'nature', 'evolution' and 'natural selection', for example. Such words as 'Fate' and 'Destiny' are sometimes cast in the same role.

'Chance' processes in evolution do not rule out divine purpose. Their role has appeared in a new light following recent discoveries in biology. Far from life being an unlikely outcome of chance processes, one biologist, Manfred Eigen, has argued:

"The evolution of life . . . must be considered an *inevitable* process despite its indeterminate course . . . it is not only inevitable 'in principle' but also sufficiently probable within a realistic span of time."

The subtle interplay between 'chance' and 'law' seems to have played an important part in the living world being as it is.

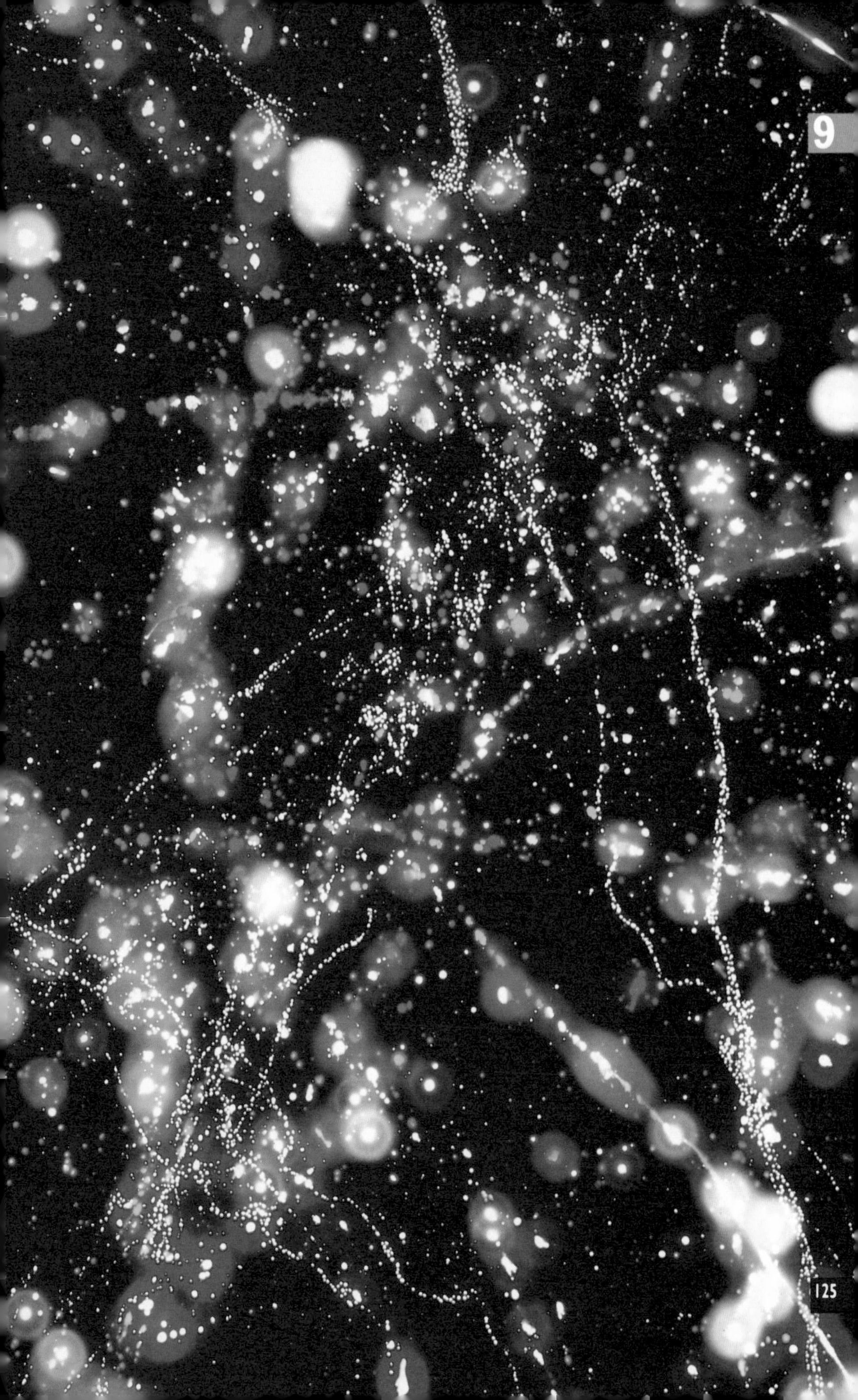

9 A CREATED WORLD

The book of Genesis opens on the positive note that the world is the work of one God, who created it for a purpose. This book will close on a similar note.

Genesis was addressed to people who, like us, were constantly bombarded by contrary views about the origins and ownership of the world. It called for responsible management of the earth and its resources under the guidance of God. Part of this management now involves science and technology. Like any other form of service, it can be done to the glory of God or not, as was recognized in the second Charter of the Royal Society. There the Fellows were commanded to direct their studies 'to the glory of God the Creator, and the advantage of the human race'.

Public opinion about science ranges between making it into a god, and despising it. Some people have regarded science as the sole means to peace and prosperity on earth. But, when the god failed to deliver the goods, they despised it. To treat science as a secular substitute for God is not only naive, it is idolatry. To abuse it because it fails to provide the solution to the world's ills is childish. It compares with the infant who kicks its toy because it will not do something for which it was never designed. Between these two extremes lies the rosy-spectacled view that, although science and technology have caused a lot of problems, they will also be the means of solving them.

Science and technology are the activities of imperfect people. The tendencies to misuse and exploit for personal gain operate here as in every other department of life. But the answer to abuse is not disuse, but responsible use.

"Not until the power conferred by our knowledge has been recognized as God's gift, enabling his children to grow up into fully developed men and women;

. . . not until man's patient observation of the world around has led him on to awe and then to worship;

not until our science has shown us with what rich lustre the heavens declare the glory of God, and the firmament shows his handiwork;

not until then can human faith be as it was meant to be, nor human life fulfil its proper destiny . . . nor our hearts be so astonished at the splendour of God's creation that they grasp eternity in a moment of time, and are lost in wonder, love and praise."

Professor Charles Coulson

Acknowledgments

Graphics by Tony Cantale Graphics, except page 107, which is by Fred Apps.

The photos are used by permission of the following:

Barnaby's Picture Library 69
Bridgeman Art Library 28/29, 31, 44/45, 75, 98, 99
British Library 16
British Museum (Natural History) 97
C.M. Dixon 85
Mary Evans Picture Library 86/87
Gamma/Frank Spooner 64/65
Sonia Halliday Photographs 80
Clive Hodges 68/69
Hulton Picture Company 102 (Huxley), 114
Image Bank/David W. Hamilton 61
Mansell Collection 41, 83, 90
C. Eric Marsh 36/37 (all), 39, 74
National Maritime Museum 40
Michael Poole 42, 48 (top right and left, bottom right), 71, 108, 119
Science Photo Library 123; /Paul Shambroom 3; Hank Morgan 20; David Leah 24; Philippe Plailly 104
David Townsend 118
ZEFA 12/13, 14/15, 18, 19, 32/33, 38, 43, 48 (bottom left), 54/55, 63, 66/67, 72/73, 76, 79, 88, 95, 96 (both), 100, 101 (all), 111, 115, 116/117, 121, 125